"Sharon Hoover's *Mapping Church Missions*
facing churches today in mission, but it als
insights to help churches better steward b
I've had the privilege of seeing Sharon apply these principles in her church and see
the impact of strategic conversations and intentional action in the life of a congregation committed to making a difference for the kingdom in today's world."
Alan B. MacDonald, global partnership facilitator at Wycliffe Bible Translators, USA

"Congregations are engaging in mission more directly, mobilizing themselves as institutions and mobilizing their members as individuals for service at home and far
away. As they do, they face new challenges and the need for new discernment.
Hoover recognizes that a church's best efforts can quickly be undone by a failure to
navigate tensions and false divisions that are often set up in the church. . . .
In *Mapping Church Missions*, Hoover tells stories in which her readers will recognize
themselves and the challenges they face, and she shares knowledge and wisdom that
will help mission leaders and their congregations to find their way. This is a book to
read and share with others, and the discussion questions that accompany each
chapter make it easy to study together."
Rob Weingartner, executive director, The Outreach Foundation

"'Love thy neighbor,' while a simple command, is complicated work. Just who do we
love? And how exactly? With her vast experience in church missions, Sharon Hoover
ably identifies the essential questions of the missions conversation, helping individuals and churches to clarify their unique values and resources, desires and opportunities. This book will do as much good in the world as those it sends out."
Jen Pollock Michel, author of *Teach Us to Want* and *Keeping Place*

"With insightful illustrations and questions for group discussion, *Mapping Church
Missions* provides a framework for discerning your congregation's direction in
mission. By helping to identify your unique perspectives and priorities on key
mission issues, your church can chart a course toward best practices and a clearer
strategy to grow in faithfulness to the Great Commission."
Jen Haddox, director of global engagement for ECO (a Covenant Order of Evangelical
Presbyterians)

"Sharon Hoover gives us a framework for the conversations that every church is *already* engaged in. The open and even-handed approach to these questions will be
invaluable to pastors, missions directors, and church members alike. This is a must-
read (and a must-keep-on-the-bookshelf) for any missions-minded Christian."
Richard Lee, director of church mobilization at International Justice Mission

"I love missions. Each one of God's children is called and sent to contribute to building God's kingdom. But past misdirected efforts and changing world realities have created confusion and conflicts that challenge the desire to serve for churches and ministries. Sharon Hoover, in *Mapping Church Missions*, has provided a powerful resource and strategy to guide a local church or mission-sending agency. Whether you are looking to go locally or globally, to focus primarily on the Great Commission or the great commandment, this book will help you assess the potential differences in perspective and consider the varying gifts, experiences, and passions of your people as you map out a path for your community in missions. A valuable compass!"

Judy Douglass, director of Women's Resources at Campus Crusade for Christ

"How are we to engage the world of mission without being overwhelmed? With so many needs—both locally and globally, in evangelism and service, in responding to crisis and sustaining development, and so many more—how are we to invest our time, energy, and finances? *Mapping Church Missions* helps readers navigate these critical questions by offering stories, biblical reflections, a wealth of experience, and inviting readers into a conversation that helps us find our place in the world of mission. I'm better equipped to lead my congregation after reading this book. Thank you, Sharon Hoover, for an excellent resource for both individuals and churches seeking to live out God's mission."

April Yamasaki, lead pastor of Emmanuel Mennonite Church, author of *Sacred Pauses: Spiritual Practices for Personal Renewal*

MAPPING CHURCH MISSI●NS

A C●MPASS FOR MINISTRY STRATEGY

SHARON R. HOOVER

FOREWORD BY **PAUL BORTHWICK**

IVP Books

An imprint of InterVarsity Press
Downers Grove, Illinois

InterVarsity Press
P.O. Box 1400, Downers Grove, IL 60515-1426
ivpress.com
email@ivpress.com

*InterVarsity Press® is the book-publishing division of InterVarsity Christian Fellowship/USA®, a movement of
students and faculty active on campus at hundreds of universities, colleges, and schools of nursing in the United
States of America, and a member movement of the International Fellowship of Evangelical Students. For
information about local and regional activities, visit intervarsity.org.*

*All Scripture quotations, unless otherwise indicated, are taken from The Holy Bible, New International Version®,
NIV®. Copyright © 1973, 1978, 1984, 2011 by Biblica, Inc.™ Used by permission of Zondervan. All rights reserved
worldwide. www.zondervan.com. The "NIV" and "New International Version" are trademarks registered in the
United States Patent and Trademark Office by Biblica, Inc.™*

*While any stories in this book are true, some names and identifying information may have been changed to protect
the privacy of individuals.*

Cover design: David Fassett
Interior design: Daniel van Loon
Images: © Jane_Kelly / iStock / Getty Images

ISBN 978-0-8308-4146-2 (print)
ISBN 978-0-8308-7401-9 (digital)

Printed in the United States of America ♾

*InterVarsity Press is committed to ecological stewardship and to the conservation of natural resources in all our
operations. This book was printed using sustainably sourced paper.*

Library of Congress Cataloging-in-Publication Data
Names: Hoover, Sharon R., 1961- author.
*Title: Mapping church missions : a compass for ministry strategy / Sharon R.
  Hoover.*
*Description: Downers Grove : InterVarsity Press, 2018. | Includes
  bibliographical references.*
*Identifiers: LCCN 2018017724 (print) | LCCN 2018026182 (ebook) | ISBN
  9780830874019 (eBook) | ISBN 9780830841462 (pbk. : alk. paper)*
Subjects: LCSH: Missions—Theory. | Evangelistic work. | Church work.
*Classification: LCC BV2063 (ebook) | LCC BV2063 .H655 2018 (print) | DDC
  266—dc23*
LC record available at https://lccn.loc.gov/2018017724

P	25	24	23	22	21	20	19	18	17	16	15	14	13	12	11	10	9	8	7	6	5	4	3	2	1
Y	37	36	35	34	33	32	31	30	29	28	27	26	25	24	23	22	21	20	19	18

**TO THE LORD JESUS CHRIST,
GOD ALMIGHTY, HOLY SPIRIT.**

My heart's tablet cherishes your gracious, steadfast presence.

**TO MY HUSBAND, CHRIS,
AND OUR CHILDREN, AARON AND ELISE.**

My life is beautiful and full because of you.

TO MY PARENTS, RON AND JUDY.

Your lifelong love and support will always be my most treasured gift.

CONTENTS

FOREWORD

PAUL BORTHWICK

Christie and I got into our rental car and readied ourselves for the drive to our mountain destination to celebrate our wedding anniversary. After driving a few miles, Christie said, "Um, I don't think the GPS is working; the screen says 'no signal.'"

If we were on our way to some location we had visited before, it might not have been an issue, but this was a lodge defined by the words *new*, *remote*, and *mountain*.

"What should we do?" I asked.

"I think the only option we have is this map."

Years ago, all of our driving relied on cumbersome, hard-to-fold, sometimes dated maps, but technology had taken us away from the paper map over a decade ago.

We knew our final destination; we had our map; we were together; and we prayed. As we studied the map, we realized that we could find routes that seemed longer or shorter. Some roads had dotted lines—indicating dirt roads or four-wheel-drive-only roads. A few of the roads looked more like hiking trails, and others seemed to cross small rivers. We had our map, but we were faced with multiple options.

After a number of twists and turns—plus a few U-turns and backtracking—we reached the dream mountain destination. We met others staying at the same lodge; they had taken different routes, but we all made it.

Our mountain drive story illustrates the message that Sharon addresses in *Mapping Church Missions*—the genuine challenge churches and individuals face in this twenty-first century as we try to determine the road ahead for involvement and investment in global outreach:

- *We know our ultimate destination.* God has given us the "brochure" by giving us a picture in Revelation 5:9 and 7:9 of people from every tribe, language, people, and nation worshiping the Lord Jesus. Our work in the here-and-now should be driving us towards that great multicultural worship service.

- *But there is no apparent GPS* from the heavens telling us exactly how to get there. Obviously we rely on prayer for God's direction, but few will report that the Lord answers verbally from heaven telling us, "Thou shalt verily give 35 percent to the Berserki unreached people group" or "Spend 50 percent of your time on short-term missions focused only on compassion ministry."

- *The route ahead might seem new or remote.* The speed of change, the impact of globalization, the worldwide "from everywhere to everywhere" understanding of missions, and the accessibility of so much of the world presents us with challenges and opportunities that previous generations never dreamed of.

- *So we need a map*—and this is what Sharon has done for us. She outlines the twists and turns by identifying and inviting us into a conversation concerning the issues every church faces—local outreach or global, evangelism versus social action, short-term missions versus "just send money," meeting emergency needs versus looking for long-term solutions.

- *And with the help of this map, we and our churches will get there.* Other churches might take a different route because they respond to these twist-and-turn issues differently. But they get there too—with *there* being every church doing their God-given part in working toward the picture we have in Revelation 5:9 and 7:9.

I so much wish I had this book in my hands when I served as a church missions pastor. Sharon combines her years of experience in church missions' leadership with practical stories to help every church, mission leadership team, and individual discover the way forward. She offers practical help with scenarios for self-evaluation so that we can understand where we are on the map now; and then she guides us with the questions and the "no-easy-answers" voice of an expert to point us forward.

We don't need to be afraid of the road ahead—in spite of the potential or perceived obstacles. Study the map, listen to Sharon's voice, fuel your future involvement with wisdom, and drive confidently.

INTRODUCTION

CHARTING OUR COURSE

I rounded the corner on my way to our missions committee meeting and nearly walked into one of the elders of our church. "Oh, George, I'm so sorry!" My attention had been on my notes for the meeting.

"No problem!" he responded. "This is actually good timing. I've been wanting to talk with you." His countenance morphed into business mode.

"Would you like to meet sometime next week?" I asked.

"No, this is fine." He fidgeted briefly. "I just want you to know my discomfort with these foreign mission trips. I don't think they're a good use of our money. And I'm not sure they best meet the needs of missionaries either."

I attempted to respond, but George's fervor had overtaken his usual courteous self. He continued, "I think the money for these trips would be better spent elsewhere—on food and school supplies for children in the ministry's care, for instance. Plus, we have many needs in our own country."

"George, I'd like to talk more with you about this, but I really need to get to the missions meeting." I wanted to continue the conversation, but neither the time nor the place were my first choices. "Can we set up a time to meet?"

"No need to meet. Just wanted to make sure you knew and understood my concerns. I won't be financially supporting the Costa Rica team."

George's smile returned now that he had unburdened himself. "But know that I will be praying for you and the team. Have a good meeting!"

What had just happened? The shock of the flyby lecture left me speechless. I struggled against the urge to follow George and continue the conversation. But our committee would be gathering momentarily. I turned back and headed toward the meeting.

The hallway confrontation was not my first conversation about different perspectives on church missions. Through years of serving as a church missions director, members have approached me with compelling cases for their mission visions, usually involving mission partners from previous churches. Discussions with colleagues in other churches also raised various models for missions. Speakers and authors—from Billy Graham to Ed Stetzer—have added further to my engagement with this conversation through books, articles, and seminars.

My near collision with George in the church hallway became a catalyst to move from a loosely threaded collection of missionaries to an intentional mission strategy. Millimeters below the surface smiles and casual conversations lay issues we needed to address. These issues were partly semantics, partly differing passions, and partly lack of knowledge. George's comments brought to light several of the unspoken undercurrents common to missions committees. His desire for careful stewardship of resources caused his resistance to the large expenditures needed for short-term mission projects. George also touched on the ongoing debate about local versus global engagement.

I am hardly alone in my desire to serve God well through missions and outreach. We all have passions and gifts to contribute toward God's kingdom. But fulfilling the Great Commission to go and make disciples gets entangled with personalities, passions, and misunderstandings. Without even knowing it, we begin to develop personal philosophies for missions—filters that help us process the overload of information.

Amid the passions and good intentions, we can easily spiral into unproductive conversations, forgetting that much more is at stake than our personal interests and agendas. When the church hops around to follow the latest mission trends, or the most charismatic missionary, or the voices of the loudest church members, the potential for intentional strategic direction decreases. Paralysis sets in when decisions become difficult. What are the best practices for balancing local and global efforts? What partnerships align with the vision of the congregation and the talents of its members? How do we assess who to support?

WITNESSES OR WANDERERS?

Amanda put three cans of green beans, toilet paper, and diapers in the food pantry's collection box in the church lobby. She stopped to talk with an elder, Mike, about coordinating the collection of school supplies for children of impoverished families in the community. After strategizing with Mike about how best to get the word out about the school supplies to a busy congregation, Amanda stopped by the missions table to get a flyer for next summer's mission trip to Kenya. Just as she left the building, she crossed paths with Megan, who was selling fair-trade jewelry. Amanda's necklace collection was already overflowing from previous purchases, each supporting women rescued from sex trafficking. But yes, she would come to Megan's jewelry party next week.

Despite her monthly donations to an international refugee agency and a missionary in Bolivia, Amanda felt guilty as she threw away mail asking for financial donations to cancer research. Television commercials about children with cleft palates caused her to reach for the mute button on the remote control. Web ads and television commercials of dogs in abusive homes added pressure to her overburdened, empathetic heart. After a particularly guilt-ridden week, Amanda wondered whether her actions changed anyone's life for the better.

I have lost count of the number of people who have told me how similar their missional engagement is to Amanda's story. This broad approach to kingdom work introduces people to the abundant needs but it does not result in meaningful connection. Despite hoping to make a significant difference, their attention instead moves rapidly from one outreach partner to another.

Are Amanda's efforts—and those of many people like her—more like serial dating? Kent Annan, codirector of Haiti Partners, likens this missions approach to flirting, bouncing from romance to romance: "When someone behaves this way in his teens or early twenties, we shake our heads and figure he'll mature. If he keeps flipping through relationships into his thirties and forties, the immaturity starts to look pathological." Surely the church can find a better way to connect God's people with the world's spiritual and physical needs.

Sometimes our congregants may know their passions, but ways to serve according to those passions remain elusive. Ministries beckon from all directions. Amidst the many worthy causes, intentionality is lost. Tragically, the noise crowds out God's voice. So, instead of serving and giving where the Spirit leads them, our members often serve when the calendar has space and give when the bank account allows.

At any moment in the day, we can look around us and find abundant physical, mental, and spiritual needs. Which way should we step? Toward the friend who struggles with depression? The neighbor who does not know Christ? The man on the corner with the "Will Work for Food" sign? The AIDS orphan in last night's news story? The three billion people unreached by the gospel message? The new missionary family trying to raise monthly support?

As followers of Christ, we recognize serving as a critical part of our spiritual journey. Yet we lose years in the ongoing search for the best ways to connect. Ample opportunities exist to explore God's call to missional engagement, but the pursuit overwhelms. It's like staring at a compass but still not knowing which way to go. Life's busyness, our lack of knowledge, and persuasive voices all around us complicate the search. Furthermore, the global landscape of missions is ever changing. New expressions of ministry emerge almost daily. Political and cultural dynamics open and close opportunities as fast as a revolving door.

Both congregants and churches alike intend to serve with purpose, but experiences rather than research tend to drive our models for ministry. Friends, agencies, and random emails invite us to join them to influence the world in the name of Jesus Christ. Soon scattered volunteer hours and random impersonal donations form our approach to missions. Each new missions opportunity merely adds to a collection of temporal outings. Our primary role as witnesses for Christ gets buried under the clutter of good intentions.

EARLY IMPRESSIONS

For many years food drives and distant missionaries shaped my perception of church missions. As a child of an army officer, I grew up in military chapels and various Protestant churches. I remember bringing canned cranberry sauce and stuffing mix for holiday food baskets. We took our hand-me-down coats to clothes closets. We prayed regularly for missionaries in the faraway lands of Africa and China. The "Today's Missionary" paragraph in Sunday bulletins captured my attention each week. Their family pictures with exotic backdrops transported me to unfamiliar corners of the planet. In my mind, missionaries always sat under sprawling shade trees, encircled by smiling villagers, absorbing Bible story after Bible story. No one ever had to gather firewood, haul water, or face injustices.

In the 1970s new worship songs began trickling into the church. The more casual lyrics touched my teenage soul in a way the old hymns missed. It awakened me to the relevance of faith in Christ. But I lacked guidance for next steps. The precept to "love your neighbor" meant to be kind and bake casseroles. The command to "go and make disciples" equaled inviting friends to church so the pastor could do the real invitation into the kingdom. The wall between world missions and local outreach was tall and wide. Personal contact with global partners was limited to furlough schedules and prayer requests. We never visited a missionary in the field.

In the 1980s and '90s, awareness of missions increased. A stirring began within the church to prioritize missional engagement. The focus on missions reached unprecedented heights. From the 1974 International Congress on World Evangelism commitment to unreached people groups, to the expansion of conferences, university study majors, and professional journals, the influence of missions was on the rise. Newsletters, biographies, and memoirs by missionaries became more widely available. Congregations became more knowledgeable about ministry in the field. Ease of travel made missionaries more accessible to supporting churches.

Opportunities opened for people to join mission partners for short-term projects. My first mission trip was with a team in 1983 to New York City's Harlem neighborhood. We worked with members of a new church plant to help refurbish an abandoned brownstone, which would eventually become their new worship center. The relationship of short-term teams during those early years focused on the missionary and their church partners. No organizations existed to facilitate trips. Within another decade, however, the number of short-term teams exploded along with the number of agencies that facilitated opportunities to serve. Churches, particularly youth ministries, were seeking increased opportunities for crosscultural mission projects. Long-term outcomes and collaborative efforts within the body of Christ, however, rarely came to the attention of the local missions committees.

Paradigm-shifting books of the early 2000s raised awareness of the unintended but growing disconnect between Christ-followers and the transformative mission of God. Richard Stearn's *The Hole in Our Gospel* confronted the Western church about its inaction toward extreme global poverty. He challenged believers to live out the whole gospel by developing relationships with the world's neediest people. Steve Corbett and Brian Fikkert's *When Helping Hurts* and Robert Lupton's *Toxic Charity* caused the church to rethink local outreaches and their effect on the people served. The books cited multiple studies depicting harm caused by charitable giving. The resulting dependency and loss of dignity prevented lasting development in impoverished communities. The conversation created by these books spread into valuable dialogue regarding crosscultural missions, both locally and globally. The church needed to clarify the role of missions in proclaiming God's kingdom here on earth.

While the call to be God's verbal witnesses and his physical presence has stayed the same, rapidly evolving technology, globalization, and entrepreneurship have expanded options for today's missional engagement. The changing landscape presents unprecedented opportunity. The swift pace, however, also increases the potential for inadvertent damage. When pursuing ministry without a well-developed strategy, we overlook important factors such as the culture and traditions of the communities we hope to serve.

MISSIONAL ENGAGEMENT ROLES

Church leaders engage missions on two separate levels. On an institutional level, we decide with whom to partner. We choose the missionaries and mission organizations to support with financial assistance, intercessory prayer, publicity, and sending people to serve. On an individual level, we help members step into their call to serve. We present a wide range of opportunities to explore possibilities. The church's day to serve with a home repair ministry, for example, provides a preplanned event for participation. As congregants labor, they discover the world's needs as well as a place to begin discerning their place in God's global mission. Both levels require our attention as we develop roles for missional engagement.

Institutional mobilization. Boards, teams, staffs, committees—whatever they may be called—gather in local churches to make decisions regarding missions partners. Men and women called into this role connect missionaries with the resources of the church. They establish a listening relationship with missionaries and connect the congregation with the global church. Healthy conversation within a missions committee is essential to responding effectively to the needs of the mission field. A well-defined missions strategy creates a safe place for collaborative thinking. Instead of a missions ministry driven by voices of the loudest team members or the missionaries with the best promotional materials, church leaders know their calling and are committed to its fulfillment.

Whenever a missions committee gathers, however, the potential for friction exists. People prioritize the world's injustices and brokenness differently. A wide variety of silent opinions enter the room with every meeting. One person's heart for evangelism emerges as concern for unreached people in isolated Himalayan villages while another person's heart for evangelism cries for the local teen lost in the trappings of alternative religions. Or what about concern for racial reconciliation? Does it carry greater weight than concern for the victims of human trafficking? When one person's agenda becomes the driving force behind an entire church's missions strategy, however, we lose the value of the full body of Christ. While we share the common goal of kingdom work for God's glory, without a common strategy our long-term effectiveness falters.

Committee members also may disagree on methods and practices to accomplish missions objectives. I have seen two church members, both passionate about sharing the gospel with people in remote villages, in fierce disagreement. One member believed in the traditional approach of sending a US missionary, while the other member was deeply committed to partnering with native missionaries to connect with the same unreached people group. Or consider how casual conversation leading to spiritual discussion in a local coffee shop stirs excitement for one evangelist, while the potential of a large tent revival moves the heart of another evangelist.

These pulls in different directions create tension within the local church. They affect everything from budget decisions to time allotted for verbal announcements in worship services. The church has the responsibility to be good stewards of each dollar entrusted to it. We agree on our call to reach a hurting and lost world, but personal agendas and contrasting definitions of missions complicate the distribution of the church's abundant resources. The North American church gave over seven hundred billion dollars to Christian causes in 2015. The distribution of the church treasury is never simple. We bear the responsibility to establish a well-thought-out missions strategy to put our resources to the best use possible.

Individual mobilization. God calls every believer to kingdom work. The roles, however, vary widely. When the church proactively educates and presents trustworthy opportunities to serve, members will begin to discern the compass bearing that best aligns with their gifts and passions. For some it's to support an organization as a donor or volunteer. For others it may be to serve as a full-time missionary—whether in a short-term capacity or as a career commitment. God works through each role to advance his global mission.

Most believers will serve God's kingdom in or near their local neighborhoods in a support role. Church-run organizations, faith-based agencies, government programs, and secular nonprofits care for families struggling with chronic poverty, men and women in prisons, those with disabilities, and other marginalized people. Supporting their work benefits the agencies, the people they serve, and God's kingdom. Many organizations are dependent on the hours given by volunteers. While serving in the community, we become aware of unmet needs. The Lord may even prompt us to begin a new initiative. A twenty-eight-year-old sales marketer in Washington, DC, for example, organized a clothing drive for professional attire when she learned that homeless men and women missed job interviews because they lacked appropriate clothing.

Many individuals and churches play important support roles for career missionaries. Whether the mission partner serves in another country or the next city over, prayer and financial support from the larger body of Christ are necessary. Through partnership, we essentially join their mission. Newsletters and emails keep supporters updated on their work. Some organizations welcome visitors and short-term teams to assist with specific ministry goals, such as leading children's camps, hosting medical missions, or helping set up micro-businesses. The support role in missions engagement cannot be overlooked or underestimated.

But God also calls some into full-time missionary service. The commitment may be for a summer, a two-year term, or an entire career. Not so long ago, Christians who entered any full-time mission service did so through the care and preparation of their church denomination. Decentralized church movements and globalization have profoundly changed the options for global missions. Mainline denominations (Presbyterians, Methodists, etc.) do continue to train and send missionaries; however, independent mission agencies send more men and women to the field.

People considering full-time missions search lists of organizations to find one that best aligns with their theology, ministry gifts, and geographic interests. Nondenominational agencies such as Operation Mobilization (OM), Pioneers, and numerous smaller organizations are equally effective in the preparatory work and care of career missionaries as traditional mission boards. They provide financial accountability, a United States–based point of contact, ongoing training, and experienced on-field supervision. Another growing trend is the blend of churches with mission agencies. The church serves as the sending body and the partner mission agency functions as the facilitator and trainer. This model reduces duplication of efforts while providing the best care and resources for those called to serve.

Another shift in the landscape of career mission service is the scope of work being pursued. While some people continue to sense God's call to traditional house-to-house evangelism and church planting, others pursue ministries focused on specific issues of justice and poverty, such as rescuing victims from human trafficking or providing shelter to refugees. Still more ministries create business-as-mission enterprises such as language schools or local manufacturing to be Christ's light in the community. Through innovative enterprises, relationships form and the gospel message weaves naturally into daily conversations and business engagements.

This book sorts out the differences and clarifies options in the complex missions landscape. We want to make wise choices to serve the unreached, the vulnerable, and the unloved in the name of Jesus. The number of options is enormous. Some people set out with the best of intentions, only to find exhaustion and discouragement from an undefined mission. Others struggle to align their abilities and their church's contribution with a long-term strategy. Our ability to join God's work gets bogged down when we are unable to step constructively into these conversations.

How do we discover the best approaches to reach the unknown and forgotten peoples with the gospel? How do the gifts and passions of a congregation contribute to the broad expression of missions? How do we evaluate the credibility and effectiveness of a potential mission partner? The questions paralyze our ability to respond well. Let's reframe the confusion into continuums that will sort the issues into manageable groups. As we wrestle through the issues, we will be able to fine-tune the direction that best aligns with God's call for each of us.

SEVEN CONVERSATIONS

As we travel this life, we have the freedom to pass through vast areas of terrain, giving our time and efforts as needed. This book will help reduce our meandering. With an improved sense of direction, we will be able to navigate the terrain and improve our ability to serve well.

It's time to pick up a compass and choose an intentional navigational bearing for our missions ministries. We need to do the hard work of discernment to discover the best path to serve. With increased understanding of the options, we hone our compass skills and improve our ability to align gifts and passions with God's calling. The church and her members will then be able to pursue effective missional engagement as closely as following a compass bearing in the wilderness. We then move from haphazard steps toward a strategic plan in God's mission to reach our neighbors, near and far.

Having participated in numerous off-sites and Saturday morning strategic planning sessions, I have found a fundamental step often rushed or missed altogether in the meetings. Prior to developing a vision statement, core values, or strategic intentions, it's critical to discuss personal points of view and unseen agendas. Sometimes we are not aware of our perspectives until discussions bring them to the fore. False assumptions, fears, and insecurities emerge and can derail even the most productive meetings. In addition, establishing a common vocabulary is an essential step toward reducing misunderstandings in the dialogue. Terms such as *people group*, *unengaged,* and even *outreach* carry different meanings to different people. Time and effort spent in this critical exploration stage allows a smoother development and implementation of a missions strategy.

This book invites conversation across seven specific topics. These topics provide a systematic overview of the issues most likely to cause conflict when developing a missions strategy. By exploring the wide range of ministry options, these topics will generate discussion pivotal to effective missional engagement. Increased familiarity with the possibilities—and the potential friction between them—provides valuable guidance for charting a church's course and allowing us to get our missional bearings. Each topic represents a continuum:

- good news and good deeds
- local and global
- crisis response and sustainability
- time and money
- benefit and harm of short-term teams
- recipient-focused and servant-focused
- the role of risk

Worthwhile ministry takes place throughout each continuum. Differences in our gifts and abilities allow for a wide variety of responses. However, some choices are better than others in certain situations. In addition, some crossover between issues will emerge in the chapters. For example, for effective good works we need to consider the crisis response and sustainability aspect of ministry to prevent damaging consequences. As you ponder the topics, you will discover the best route to get to your missional destination. As a compass helps navigate unfamiliar territory, each conversation steers your choices. You will explore a host of possibilities to discern your church's divinely appointed role in the kingdom. You will turn a loosely connected assortment of commitments into a focused missions strategy.

GOOD NEWS AND GOOD DEEDS

We had gathered food for weeks. Finally, the day arrived to prepare the Thanksgiving baskets. The hallway off the church lobby was busier than the New York subway as the assembly line formed to sort canned vegetables, fresh fruit, and holiday treats. We loaded cars and fanned out into the community to deliver baskets to at-risk families.

On that very day, however, one woman's statement brought the decade-long tradition to an abrupt halt.

"Oh, I knew the president would come through for us this year," she exclaimed as our members carried bags of food into her home. She genuinely believed the groceries had come from federal public assistance.

In a most gracious tone, yet through clenched teeth, one of our deliverers clarified that the gift was from God and not from the government. He was quick to point out elected officials were not involved in the holiday blessings.

The discussion continued into our church hallways. Questions flew but the answers were few. Why do we provide food? What about sharing faith? But then, how does the gospel message matter when a family is in need of basic sustenance? Are there other ways to address poverty in our community? What is the best use of resources when the church alone serves as the verbal witnesses for the gospel? We wrestled with these questions over and over. They not only influenced our missions strategy but also forced us to examine our personal philosophies of evangelism and outreach.

The first of seven conversations for discovering our compass bearing for missional engagement centers on the verbal expression of faith. The continuum ranges from good works with no spoken or written faith component to evangelistic outreaches whose sole purpose is the verbal presentation of the gospel. This dichotomy fuels an undercurrent of disagreement among Christ-followers. For some people the purposes are mutually exclusive.

On one end of the continuum the focus of missional engagement is deeds. Whether feeding the poor or caring for our planet, the efforts seek to alleviate suffering and to establish a hospitable world. On the other end the focus of missional engagement is sharing the good news. Through the written or spoken word, evangelists communicate the message of hope and healing through restoration of relationship with God.

Where does your missional engagement compass point—toward doing good deeds or telling the good news? To determine our compass bearing, we will examine both ends of the continuum as well as options in between. Believers are called to give voice to the message of salvation for all who have not heard. But without adequate food and water, there is no one to hear the story!

As we enter this conversation, resist the urge to place a value judgment on either end of the continuum. Recognize your leaning toward one end or the other as your personal preference rather the "right" way for everyone. The potential for good—and for harm—exists at both ends of the continuum. This conversation will be most fruitful where it helps us discover new possibilities for kingdom work. With open minds and soft hearts, let's wade into the first conversation.

CALLED TO GOOD DEEDS

Response to the needs of others was deeply rooted in the early church. Followers of Jesus shared food, shelter, and possessions (Acts 2:44; 4:32-37).

No one lacked basic sustenance. The importance of daily food distribution drove the early church to make its first organizational decision. The apostles appointed seven disciples to care for impoverished widows (Acts 6:1-4). The early believers' care for one another was so revolutionary it caught the attention of Jews and Gentiles alike. The community of believers revealed God's nature of love and grace in their compassionate care for one another. The church multiplied rapidly as more people wanted to be part of the Christian family of faith.

Today benevolence organizations continue to alleviate suffering for those unable to meet their own needs. Services such as English as a second language (ESL) classes, health clinics, and assistance for people with disabilities provide critical resources for at-risk people in our communities.

These selfless acts of kindness and goodness bring the Lord's presence into a hurting world. Our actions serve as testimony to Christ within us (Galatians 5:22). When we bring a meal to a sick neighbor, or donate school supplies for refugee children, or visit those in prison, the Lord himself is there. As Eric Swanson and Rick Rusaw put it, "Mercy is God's attitude and action toward people in distress." As the Spirit prompts and gives us strength, we respond to the needs of others with God's mercy.

While exploring paths to serving others, one factor we might consider is religious affiliation. Both Christian and non-Christian agencies care for vulnerable populations across the globe. There are disaster response agencies that are faith-based, such as Samaritan's Purse, and those that are not, such as the Red Cross. Both agencies are able to mobilize quickly and care for physical needs, which makes them effective first responders in crisis situations. Similarly, both Lawyers Without Borders and International Justice Mission (IJM) provide pro bono counsel to address justice issues worldwide. Both organizations are nonprofits and have received accolades for their work, but only IJM has a faith foundation.

Christ-followers give time regularly to care for needs within their own communities. Some invest in their neighborhoods as reading buddies, elder caregivers, or coaches. Although few of these opportunities are faith based, schools and youth sports benefit from the many hours given. Mentors of all ages and stages of life offer support needed to encourage personal growth and development.

Our definition of good deeds also needs to include the work of Christians advocating for increased care of our environment. The Lord formed a breathtaking planet, called it "good," then placed its stewardship in our care. We bear the responsibility for the animals, plants, oceans, and the very air we breathe. Yet daily we hear stories of pollution, extinction, and callous disregard of natural resources. When hiking on the Appalachian Trail, my husband and I met two young men who serve on a volunteer trail crew. They had anonymously given hundreds of hours to maintain and improve the East Coast trail. This kind of valuable work allows you and me to better enjoy God's gift of nature and to do good for God's created world.

Some believers, however, question the hours spent on these pursuits. With the many people who do not yet know Christ, isn't attending to social justice a distraction from the greater need to save souls? The Bible, however, does not support the separation of body and soul. God created the universe, including human beings, and called it all good. Jesus walked the earth fully divine and fully human. His bodily presence, followed by his physical resurrection, attests to the reality of our united body and soul.

Attempts to divide and rank body and soul have pervaded the church since its earliest days. Gnostic dualism asserted the insignificance of the body compared to the eternal value of the soul. We find these ideas today creeping into the church through some New Age mystical practices that encourage adherents to attain the hidden truths and deeper knowledge of God. Among the implications of this philosophy is the reduced importance of caring for the physical needs of self and others. It marginalizes the body and the world, diminishing the worth of good deeds.

We become spiritually alive in Christ through grace alone: no special knowledge required. Doing good is intimately connected with our spiritual journey. "For we are God's handiwork, created in Christ Jesus to do good works, which God prepared in advance for us to do" (Ephesians 2:10).

Escaping physical existence to experience salvation is incompatible with the whole gospel of Jesus Christ. Saving souls is intimately connected with social justice. "Religion that God our Father accepts as pure and faultless is this: to look after orphans and widows in their distress" (James 1:27).

Some people come to faith in Christ after first witnessing the selfless acts of his followers. Their path may be long and winding, but the general direction is toward physical and spiritual healing. Good deeds minister to heart, soul, mind, *and* body.

Lost in addiction and homelessness, Carl walked into the soup kitchen. It was a repurposed storefront. He carried cynicism and anger along with his ragged, overstuffed backpack. Warm food and strong coffee welcomed him that morning. And the next. And the next. As the weeks moved on, Carl formed friendships with other guests and the staff. He began attending the AA meetings and occasionally took a seat at the Wednesday afternoon Bible study.

Carl had stepped onto the path of recovery. But it had taken a safe entry place with no motive other than to meet his most basic physical needs. The breakfast casseroles and lunch sandwiches donated daily from local churches and community groups made a difference. Carl repeatedly tells of the generous and welcoming staff—paid and volunteer—who drew him up from his darkest pit. He recognized God's presence through the benevolent care given. As the apostle John reminds us, "If anyone has material possessions and sees a brother or sister in need but has no pity on them, how can the love of God be in that person?" (1 John 3:17).

When serving to meet physical needs, moments may arise when faith enters into the narrative. Sometimes appeals for help or prayer requests arise. A public-school mentor recounted a conversation with a teacher: "Mrs. Smith asked if our church has a youth group. She is struggling with some issues with her son. We talked in the hall about parenting and church." Another church member who coaches basketball shared, "Joe asked me to pray for his dad. He is having heart surgery next week." Discussions begin spontaneously about the hardships of life. Serving shoulder to shoulder with not-yet-believers makes the church more approachable. As unmet needs inch toward resolution, the perseverance and compassion of Christ-followers bring glory to God and create the space for people to encounter him without pretense. Without expectation of first hearing the good news, unmerited service turns up grace-filled encounters.

CALLED TO GOOD NEWS

Just as political ambassadors represent their country's interests and policies as the personal designates of their own heads of state, so we are God's representatives who carry his kingdom message: "We are therefore Christ's ambassadors, as though God were making his appeal through us" (2 Corinthians 5:20). Stunning. The King entrusted his message of grace and salvation to us, his royal subjects.

In a bold and seemingly reckless decree, Jesus empowered believers to deliver his message. "All authority in heaven and on earth has been given to me," Jesus told his disciples after his resurrection. "Therefore go and make disciples of all nations, baptizing them in the name of the Father and of the Son and of the Holy Spirit" (Matthew 28:18-19). This mandate of evangelism, now known as the Great Commission, remains a central tenet in the faith of every Christ-follower. In every tribe and tongue we tell the message that Jesus Christ is alive, and through his sacrificial death we can stand before God the Father without sin, shame, or fear. Central to our calling is proclamation.

On this earthly journey we will be called on to bear witness to our heavenly home and the King of kings. But has our voice gone silent? Many believers have expressed concern that the church has forgotten her call to evangelism. Ed Stetzer notes that "in relating God's mission, the message increasingly includes the hurting but less frequently includes the global lost. . . . It is ironic, though, that as many missional Christians have sought to 'embody' the gospel, they have chosen to forsake one member of Christ's body: the mouth." It is a grave error to neglect this part of the body.

Whether because of a lack of urgency or an aversion to potentially risky conversation, we shy away from the verbal expression of the gospel. Andy Crouch suggests that

meeting the physical needs of the poor wins attention and affirmation from a watching world. Naming the spiritual poverty of a
world enthralled to false gods provokes defensiveness and derision
from those who do not even believe there is a god. Disaster relief and
economic development seem like achievable goals that bring people
together; religious claims to know the one true God seem like di-
visive mysteries that drive people apart. . . . In short, working for
justice is cool. Proclaiming the gospel is not.

Yet when we bring the life-giving words of the gospel message, we speak
into the need of the lost soul. Do we lack Paul's boldness, who declared, "I
am not ashamed of the gospel, because it is the power of God that brings
salvation to everyone who believes: first to the Jew, then to the Gentile"
(Romans 1:16)? The good news of Jesus Christ heralds the arrival of a new,
all-encompassing kingdom. Yet our obsession with not offending people
with the gospel insults the very nature of the message. The Spirit prompts
but our tongues remain silent. How many of us cower behind the facade
of good deeds when good words beg to be spoken?

Physical needs do indeed exist in the world today. But as pastor and
author John Rackley writes,

> Christian mission should not mistake itself for a humanitarian relief
> agency. This is a disconcerting thought. Many Christians and
> churches act as if the gospel is solely about what we can do to re-
> spond to the words of Jesus in Luke 4:16-23 ("The Spirit of the Lord
> is on me, because he has anointed me to proclaim good news to the
> poor. He has sent me to proclaim freedom for the prisoners and re-
> covery of sight for the blind, to set the oppressed free." Luke 4:18).

The tendency to prioritize freedom for the prisoner and sight for the blind
overlooks Jesus' calling to preach the good news.

When we favor serving the physically poor over the spiritually poor, we
diminish the call to restored relationship with God. Reconciliation with

God emerges from the choice to follow and worship God. But "how, then, can they call on the one they have not believed in? And how can they believe in the one of whom they have not heard? And how can they hear without someone preaching to them?" (Romans 10:14). We are vocal ambassadors of this message, not merely demonstrators.

Social responsibility does indeed call the church to awareness of physical needs. Yet when church missions and the Peace Corps become indistinguishable, the legitimacy of our approach is called into question. As the church's salvific message becomes marginalized, we cease fulfilling the biblical mandate to spread the good news. Do community initiatives without the gospel truly demonstrate God's love? Does a focus on ensuring today's lunch and tonight's bed overlook the message of eternal hope in Jesus Christ?

Recognizing the theological commitments of our denominational traditions may offer insight into why we lean toward one end of the continuum or the other. More progressive traditions have tended to focus on social justice, while conservatives have emphasized intellectual orthodoxy. Author and Cru staff Randy Newnan notes that in the early to mid-1900s, the expression of the gospel in more liberal congregations turned toward food and clothing distribution, prison outreach, and other expressions of mercy, while the more fundamentalist congregations dedicated themselves to leading people to a saving faith in God through Jesus Christ.

While God calls all believers to tell the gospel message, he has specially anointed some believers to be evangelists of his story (Ephesians 4:11-12). Undaunted and impassioned, they lead people to Christ through inspired preaching and teaching. While ministry models vary widely among evangelists, they remain committed to the clear and effective communication of God's sacrificial offer of eternal life.

Over the years God sparked revolutionary spiritual revivals through his evangelists. From Jonathan Edwards's preaching and William Carey's missionary work of the 1700s to the present-day ministries of Luis Palau, evangelists have shared the gospel message in large city stadiums and modest church sanctuaries. As a young teen, my husband was one of the countless souls who knelt in front of their televisions while Rev. Billy Graham, a thousand miles away, led him to faith in Christ. It was Aimee Semple McPherson in the early 1900s who actually opened the way for modern-day televangelists. She founded the Foursquare Church and was one of the first to use media to share the gospel. Although her life was a controversial one, few would argue against her visionary use of radio for kingdom purposes.

If the spiritual needs of others tug on your heart or the hearts of your church leaders, there are numerous options for you to explore. Church planting remains a high priority for many established churches. This may be accomplished through a traditional daughter church, where a pastor-evangelist and a handful of families from the parent church establish a new location. A rising number of church plants, however, use a multisite strategy. Video technology links campuses together on Sunday mornings and other meeting times, though typically each site has its own campus pastor to build relationships and lead the community in that particular location. Some multisite church plants are in the next town while others are a continent away.

Church planting among unreached people groups remains a priority in the mainline denominational efforts of Baptists, Methodists, and Presbyterians. Smaller independent agencies, such as Frontier Fellowship, also prioritize their outreach toward the seven thousand ethnic groups who have not yet heard the gospel message. In remote and less accessible regions, some Christ-followers carry the gospel through business-as-mission (BAM) entrepreneurship. Language schools, coffee shops, stove factories, and textile operations show the love of Christ through distinctive practices. Integrity, fair trade, and human-rights practices open doors for conversation about faith and the good news of Jesus Christ.

In locations hostile to God's Word, media ministries offer one of the best opportunities to share the gospel. Internet and radio outreach, for example, allow Afghan Christian Media to proclaim the gospel in Afghanistan and

Pakistan. Founder Hussain Andaryas's knowledge of the local Dari language and culture enable him to connect with people from the security of US soil. Another viable option is to partner with native-born evangelists. Agencies such as Advancing Native Missions and Living Bread connect Western churches with indigenous pastors and missionaries working among the global poor. Familiarity and comfort with life in marginalized communities allows the living expenses of indigenous church planters to be less than what would be needed to host a Western missionary.

Some people with the gift of evangelism have a heart for a specific age group. The ministries of Cru, InterVarsity, and Young Life focus on students in high school and college. Staff members raise their own financial and prayer support. Other agencies devote efforts to sharing the gospel with younger children. Child Evangelism Fellowship, for example, developed the Good News Club as a way to evangelize and disciple elementary-age children after school. They equip and encourage volunteers to create and maintain clubs in local schools. Other organizations, such as Alpha, aim to create a safe environment for adult seekers to explore the big questions of life and faith.

Not-yet-believers include those who have never heard the name of Jesus as well as hardhearted people who have not heeded his call. Whether the unreached man of the Amaruwa tribe in Columbia or the work-consumed businesswoman in New York City, each soul is precious to God. We are obedient when we share the gospel. In the renewal of the church, development and justice cannot come at the expense of the good news.

FINDING OUR PLACE

Can we be both community volunteers and kingdom laborers? Yes. The reality of it lies in the condition of the heart. When we sense a prompting to serve in a way that glorifies God and loves others, we would be disobedient not to explore it further. But there is no stretchy kingdom garment that fits every scenario. Communities need God's healing presence in all areas. Injustice burdens the weak and the vulnerable. Souls wander in spiritual darkness. Nature cries out. The complexity of physical and spiritual needs requires a multifaceted response to advance the kingdom message.

The discord created by valuing one end of the continuum over the other weakens the witness of all believers. Ministry happens throughout the continuum. Yet personal opinions and unspoken biases influence too many discussions in this conversation. When our definition of a kingdom laborer is shaped by the Scriptures, we will find common goals even among the most diverse forms of kingdom work. We will be able to move forward together.

The greatest challenge in finding our place in this continuum emerges from the division between sacred and secular. Church leaders tend to place higher value on all things sacred, often without realizing it. For example, the tablecloth used for the communion table rarely doubles as a table covering for the church picnic of hot dogs and hamburgers. The occupational choice to become a pastor or missionary is revered and celebrated in the Sunday morning worship service, but when did we last celebrate a college student's choice to be an engineer? Sacred is spiritual and eternal while secular is physical and temporal. In our desire to live holy lives, we want to invest time and effort in activities we perceive as sacred and eternal.

But the sacred-secular division has done great harm to the cause of the church. The distinction draws us into ranking activities and ministries as we value the sacred callings—serving the church and Christian organizations—more than callings into society, business, and government. The propensity toward the sacred suggests that God calls the worthiest people into Christian service. One ministry leader told me it was acceptable for the church to lead an after-school club focused on sharing the gospel, but mentoring children or providing backpack snacks is not suitable work for the church. The resulting chasm hinders efforts to reach a hurting and broken world in a holistic way. This approach undervalues the work of Christ-followers in sectors of society outside the church.

Some believers choose secular agencies intentionally to engage people beyond Christian circles. The broader scope of relationships facilitates awareness of problems throughout the community. Furthermore, collaboration in non-Christian settings actually increases the potential for conversations with unbelievers. We simply encounter more people who do not know Christ there. No matter where we serve, our actions reflect God's presence. Regardless of the circumstances, when we demonstrate love, joy, peace, patience—along with the rest of the fruit of the Spirit— we become his presence in the world (Galatians 5:22-23). A piping-hot pot roast donated to a soup kitchen adds flavor to the lives of the poor. "Feed my sheep," Jesus told Peter (John 21:17). We cannot miss the literal meaning in this statement, nor Peter's humble desire to glorify God with the rest of his life.

How then do we best communicate the gospel? The answer is as complex as the intricate gears in a pocket watch. People, place, and situation are moving parts. Together they form challenges unique in each setting. An effective outreach in Guatemala City may not translate to success in Mumbai. The needs within two communities may lie at opposite ends of the good news–good deeds continuum. Responding to either end can both honor and advance the gospel. Our personal passion for social justice—or for telling the gospel message—cannot be the determining factor for the needs of a community. I may be an evangelist at heart, but the story of Jesus would be like static noise to the mother watching her child starve. Conversation within the community, along with prayer and the Lord's leading, will reveal the best course of action.

When we look to the One who was himself the good news, we find an array of responses from one end of the continuum to the other. To the woman bleeding, he brought physical healing. To the demoniac at Gerasene, he brought spiritual cleansing. To the hillside crowd, he brought dinner. To the tax collector Zacchaeus, he brought restoration with God and the community of faith. To the Pharisees, Jesus brought debate. His articulate words and flawless logic confounded the religious leaders until they altogether ceased approaching him. Jesus tailored his actions to each person and situation he encountered.

Following Jesus' example, context must shape our approach to serving the people who walk among us. Although we lack his divine insight into hidden wounds and motives, we serve under the guidance of the Holy Spirit. His work within their souls and our increased sensitivity to his promptings open avenues for conversations of faith. We then have the responsibility to articulate the hope we have in Jesus Christ and to invite others into fellowship with him.

I sat beside a young woman whose failed suicide attempt thankfully ended with her in a hospital bed. She talked about the dark, raw edges of her childhood. We cried together. I listened. Her voice was tenuous and soft. As gentle as a summer breeze, the Spirit whispered into my soul. Following his leading, I shared about Jesus and his message of peace and hope. Days and weeks later she and I continued the conversation about faith. Today this young woman walks with the Lord and radiates his light to people around her.

In the church lobby on another day I sat beside a young woman struggling in an abusive relationship. Winter wind rattled the back doors. Fragile from difficulties with family, job loss, and a criminal record, she quivered amid the uncertainties of the future. A tear escaped her attempts at control. In the tenderness of the moment, we talked about her physical safety. We drank hot tea. Prompted by the Spirit's tender insight, I told her we had some donated coats available if she wanted one. A nod and widened eyes affirmed her acceptance of the offer. While she waited in the lobby, I went to my office and emptied the pockets of my coat. It was the perfect size for her and it wouldn't be missed among the half-dozen other coats hanging in my hall closet at home. My young friend did indeed need Jesus, but that conversation would come at a later date. The situation shapes our approach.

Saturating the community with the gospel means we effectively connect physical, emotional, and spiritual poverty with the gospel. When the connection is tenuous, benevolence and evangelism at best become a distraction to one another, at worst they become a competition. We must share this responsibility of living and speaking the kingdom language of love and salvation. The job is far too massive for any one model. We cannot travel this road alone. Kingdom growth depends on people who plant the seed of the gospel, those who water the seed, and those who harvest the ripened plants.

With remarkable creativity Christ-followers take on these roles. Believers are at work every day in all sectors of society and throughout the world. In humility we recognize the diversity of kingdom work including both physical and spiritual needs. The support we express for one another's callings becomes an additional testimony of faith to people who do not yet know Jesus. Hand in hand we serve the world for the sake of the gospel.

We recognize good deeds as more than a means to open opportunities to share the gospel. Their ultimate end remains the same as the evangelists' message: restoration of relationship between people and God. Paul Borthwick reflects on our call to both the Great Commission and great compassion, "To stay balanced, I focus on the fact that God sees people as both loved and lost." When the church views good news and good deeds as integrated, we resist the temptation to rank them. The Lord's call on our congregations will place us at various points along this continuum. He directs us in different ways to address the different physical and spiritual needs around us.

Our churches' missional engagement can effectively emerge anywhere along the continuum. Richard Stearns reminds us that life is about the people we meet: "When we become involved in people's lives, work to build relationships, walk with them through their sorrows and their joys, live with generosity toward others, love and care for them unconditionally, stand up for the defenseless, and pay particular attention to the poorest and most vulnerable, we are showing Christ's love to those around us, not just talking about it." With attentiveness to the needs around us and to the prompting of the Holy Spirit, we become evangelists within our acts of charity *and* compassionate servants who give voice to our hope in Christ.

In his comprehensive summary, David Bosch defined evangelism as

> that dimension and activity of the church's mission which, by word and deed and in the light of particular conditions and in particular context, offers every person and community, everywhere, a valid opportunity to be directly challenged to a radical reorientation of their lives, a reorientation which involves such things as deliverance from slavery to the world and its powers; embracing Christ as Savior and Lord; becoming a living member of his community, the church; being enlisted into his service of reconciliation, peace, and justice on earth; and being committed to God's purpose of placing all things under the rule of Christ.

Our demonstration of God's love comes in word and deed. The Lord may call your church to serve the physically and spiritually lost people in a local school or in an unreached region. Through the work of discernment, the voice of the Spirit will prevail over the influence of personal preferences and strong personalities.

Whether your congregation's calling is to the unserved or the unreached, God can work through your church family to accomplish his mission. The call is quite simple: make disciples of all nations. To do so we share the good news with neighbors near and far. The gospel message, however, does not allow us to step over injustices on our way to the next unevangelized territory. Nor does it allow us to disappear behind acts of kindness when words of salvation beckon to be spoken.

QUESTIONS

1. Which one of the following scenarios best describes your place on the good news–good deeds continuum? Choose the one that most closely represents the direction of your calling. From your perspective, what makes your choice the best option?

❑ With heightened awareness of the poverty in his community, Andrew encourages his church to invest more resources in the physical needs of people. He is passionate about supporting emergency food or housing assistance needs that arise due to natural disasters or other crises. Andrew supports his church's work alongside agencies focused on longer-term needs, such as home rehab or literacy education, as well. He intentionally chooses non-faith-based organizations to reach people reluctant to seek support from Christians.

❑ Bonita seeks to serve with organizations whose primary objective is to meet the physical needs of people. The organizations may or may not have a Christian affiliation but willingly permit faith-based conversations with people receiving services.

❑ Chan Ho desires to partner with faith-based organizations who approach needs holistically. Along with meeting physical needs, he expects their resource offerings to include spiritual direction and faith-based encouragement. Chan Ho also wants their vision statement to include Christian tenets of faith.

❑ Daniella only serves with organizations who are intentional about sharing the gospel message while providing for people's physical needs. She wants her church to partner with ministries who maintain a heart for prayer and evangelism as core values.

❑ Burdened by the large numbers of people who do not know Jesus, Enrique partners with ministries whose primary objective is to evangelize. They invest minimal resources in meeting the physical needs of people. He works closely with his church leadership to equip members to share the gospel and to work with organizations with similar goals.

2. Rank the scenarios regarding the direction of God's call for your church's role in missional engagement. Which ones most represent the majority of your church's mission partnerships? Give examples to support your ranking.

3. How would you improve your church's ability to fulfill its calling in the good news–good deeds continuum?

4. What are some consequences of the sacred-secular divide in your missions settings? What changes, if any, would you recommend to further the gospel message?

NEIGHBORS NEAR AND FAR

C an we talk about the Haiti project?" Lauren stepped into my office. "Sure!" I loved it when students dropped by the church on their way home from school.

The questions came rapid fire: "How much is the deposit? How much is the total cost? And when do I need my passport?"

"The deposit is a hundred dollars. I don't know the final costs yet. We'll keep fundraising and, Lord willing, that'll cover much of the airfare and team supply fees. I'll need your passport number for the airline reservation in about a month."

"How do I get a passport?"

"The best way is through the post office. Your parents will need to help with the paperwork and gathering everything to apply."

Lauren shifted on the couch and looked away. "They don't want me to go. Actually, they said I can't go."

"Oh! Now that's something we need to discuss." Parents most frequently ask about diseases, political unrest, and other factors of risk. "Are they concerned about safety?"

"No. They said there is no reason to leave the country because we have poor people who live inside our own borders."

I nodded. "That is a bigger issue. How about the four of us getting together to chat?"

Lauren agreed enthusiastically. The meeting, however, never took place. Her parents had made their decision and were not interested in discussion. Lauren did not serve on the Haiti mission project.

Later that evening, another church member approached me.

"Did you read the article I sent you? Here's some more information about the Cambodian ministry." Steve handed me a stapled packet of papers.

"Yes, it was great to read about their work in this community!" I flipped through the additional pages of photos and newsletters. After years of little progress, whole families were now coming into the saving knowledge of Jesus Christ.

"I want to propose to the missions ministry that we send our end-of-year funding to them," Steve told me. "We need to increase our global engagement, especially toward the unreached people groups."

"Well, we're moving into our third quarter planning, so this is a good time to bring it up, Steve."

"We also need to talk about increasing our overall support for international missions. Local ministries can reach their funding goals with government assistance and state grants. Plenty of resources exist for the poor in our community." Steve's passion for global evangelism shaped his every conversation regarding missions and outreach. "What do you think about decreasing support for the local food pantry?"

Here we had two families in the same church, praying for the same gospel influence, and worshiping weekly in the same sanctuary, yet holding radically different views on the church's role in missions.

The second of the seven conversations for discovering your church's compass bearing for missional engagement centers on geography. The breadth of possibility ranges from next-door neighbors to people on the other side of the planet. These polar opposites cause much debate among mission-minded believers. The mantra of realtors—"location, location, location"—holds similar weight in the world of missions.

On one end of the continuum the focus of missional engagement is local ministry. Each day reveals material and spiritual poverty in suburbs and cities alike. Sensing God's prompting, local-centered believers are especially attentive and responsive to the needs of others in close physical proximity.

On the other end of the continuum the focus is global ministry. The highest priority is to reach people in new geographic locations with the gospel message. Deeply burdened by people groups who have not yet heard the name of Jesus, global-centered believers uproot from comfortable lives to profess God's truths in the farthest corners of the planet.

Where does your missional engagement compass point—toward local or global needs? Or some combination of the two? This chapter will explore potential routes and venture into newfound territory. Technology and diaspora ministries offer unprecedented opportunities for all peoples to hear the gospel message. The local-global distinction is beginning to blur with these new avenues of sharing the gospel.

Before we launch further into our local-global conversation, we need to clarify the use of two words: *outreach* and *missions*. Many churches refer to local ministry as outreach and global ministry as missions. The term *outreach* also carries undertones of crisis intervention and meeting physical needs. Traditionally it tends to refer to services such as food pantries and emergency rent assistance, whereas evangelism and international work are implied when using the term *missions*. However, this book uses the terms *outreach* and *missions* interchangeably. Context will distinguish between local and global, as well as between evangelism and benevolence ministry.

Of all the continuums we will discuss in this book, the local-global tension has the deepest roots in our church culture. Missional engagement in most churches is separated into the two buckets—local missions and global missions—each with their own budgets, calendars, and staff. Sincere and faithful Christ-followers dwell at both ends of the continuum and in all places in between. Let's travel the spectrum together and explore the possibilities for your church's missional engagement.

LOCAL OUTREACH

Our compass needs to point to best practices to reach our own neighborhoods. Living out faith within a local context has many expressions. Scripture calls believers to care for the people within the intimate circles of our lives: family, fellow believers, work colleagues, and neighbors. The goal, however, is to be more than the friendliest neighbor or the most supportive coworker. Our purpose remains to glorify God by obeying his commands to tell the good news and to meet the needs of others.

Jesus was not a world traveler. Aside from his childhood visit to Egypt fleeing Herod's wrath, his family resided in Nazareth. During his public ministry, he did not travel more than seventy-five miles from his hometown. Within those miles he proclaimed the gospel, brought sight to the blind, cured the lame, and fed the hungry. He was attentive to the spiritual and physical needs of the people he encountered.

We continue this calling today as Jesus instructed. "Greater love has no one than this: to lay down one's life for one's friends" (John 15:13). Following his death and resurrection, Jesus commanded his disciples to go in his authority—under the guidance of the Holy Spirit—to serve as his witnesses. Their ministry would begin with their neighbors in Jerusalem.

The book of Acts preserves the poignant story of Dorcas (Acts 9:36-43). She lived a quiet life in the port city of Joppa. Dorcas sewed robes and tunics. But she also made many of her neighbors' lives better. She was widely known for doing good deeds in her community, especially for the poor. When she became gravely ill and died, the town mourned. The believers in Joppa found Peter and urged him to come. Peter arrived and heard many accounts of Dorcas's humble, servant heart. Peter sank to his knees and prayed. Miraculously, the Lord restored Dorcas to life. Many people came to faith in Christ as Dorcas's story spread across town.

The apostle Paul's letters encouraged believers to carry one another's burdens (Galatians 6:2), help the weak (1 Thessalonians 5:14), and make the most of every conversation (Colossians 4:5-6). These words apply equally to us today. As we noted in the previous chapter, the early church's care for one another and for the vulnerable in the community drew much attention. The disciples reflected Christ's love to their neighbors and fellow tradesmen. Their actions demonstrated the local influence of Christ-centered lives.

To find our place to serve, we need to start within our own zip code. Where does your church have influence? Where do church members have a presence or a role in the community? How can you as Christ-followers speak into the gaps?

Following the drug overdose of yet another local teen, my church joined the fight against the national opioid crisis. The outpouring of grief and remorse gripped our suburban Washington, DC, community. Local government officials grappled with how to respond. Parents sought tools to protect their children. Because our church already had a presence in the local schools, we joined the conversation.

Partnering with local officials and church leaders, we helped plan a community-wide summit. The afternoon event raised awareness among parents and helped teens discover strategies to thrive beyond the toxic, drug-laden culture. Pastors, law enforcement officers, and social service providers talked with families about the realities of the growing influence of drugs. The church was a voice of hope and faith in the conversation. The positive feedback from among the four hundred participants is leading us to prepare another forum.

People come in and out of our lives as we navigate daily routines. Through these relationships we can make eternal differences in our communities. As church members explore local places to serve, encourage them to consider life's various sectors: where they live, where they work, and what interests they enjoy.

A local church's relationship with immediate neighbors reveals much about the congregation's heart for others. Whether Sunday morning services are in a suburban church building or a city storefront, relationships across shared property lines can be supportive or harmful. If peace emanated from every physical presence of the body of Christ, the world would be a profoundly different place.

Regular communication conveys our desire to be good neighbors. When planning big events at church, keep your neighbors informed of timing, as well as the potential of extra traffic and noise. These are also great opportunities to invite them to join you. Your immediate neighbors may not be your church's target audience, but they're still your neighbors. This attitude also models the welcoming posture we want our congregants to be extending in their own neighborhoods.

Consider the many connections we have with the people who live in the apartments or the houses next door to us. A chat over the fence or porch railing. A get-together for coffee or dinner. Do you have children involved in sports? Long games and metal bleachers allow many opportunities for conversation. As we learn the stories of the people around us, we discover ways to come alongside them. The Lord is able to work through your relationships when you have a voice in their lives.

One growing trend among churches with a heart for local ministry is the development of missional communities. Typically, a missional community includes about twenty to fifty people. Relationships are at the heart of these ministries as they gather for meals, prayer, Bible study, and caring for one another. But their lives together extend beyond a weekly meeting. Missional community members attend the ball games and concerts of each other's children. They show up at promotion ceremonies and anniversary parties.

Each missional community is a network of relationships intentionally serving the people in a specific geographic area. They get to know each other's friends. The missional community's outward focus emerges naturally. They talk about faith and the value of doing life together. Not-yet-believers meet Jesus along the journey but not always in traditional ways. The topic for the next Bible study, for example, is often secondary to plans for hosting the next neighborhood barbeque. The goal is building relationships as people are introduced to faith in Jesus Christ.

The second location of influence for Christ-followers is the workplace. We need not leave faith at the threshold of the church building or in our homes. Business practices of integrity, compassionate customer service, and kindness toward coworkers testify to the reality of God in our lives. The church can equip congregants to be effective witnesses for Christ in their workplace.

Christians spend significant hours working side by side with the same colleagues. As the days go by, opportunities will arise to be witnesses for Christ. Through the prompting of the Holy Spirit, and with gentleness and respect, we can guide a conversation toward spiritual topics. Offers for prayer for an ailing parent, a wayward son, or daycare struggles are rarely turned down.

Fellow believers can be invaluable colleagues at work. They can offer a Christ-centered voice, encouragement, and accountability. All over the world employees in private and government offices gather for early morning prayer and lunchtime Bible study. When coworkers from many different church backgrounds come together under the common banner of Jesus, people notice. He is glorified in the marketplace.

The third location of influence is among people with a shared area of interest. When we gather as a softball team or a book club, we begin forming relationships and engaging in conversations. Opportunities to share our faith come up when we talk about common matters like weekends and family life. "Our pastor told the funniest story on Sunday . . ." or "I'm helping my daughter pack for the summer mission trip." We need only be attentive for openings to talk about the importance of God in our lives. Our actions speak here too. Peace and kindness demonstrate our allegiance to the kingdom of God.

Ten years ago a member in our congregation had a vision to develop a community theater in our church building. She wanted to combine her heart for the Lord and her love for the arts—a beautiful ministry birthed out of her passion. By the time she retired, we had staged ten large productions. The greatest accomplishment, however, was bigger than a place for young actors and musicians to develop their talents. This community became a place for doubters to ponder faith, not-yet-believers to find genuine community, and young believers to grow.

The church builds trust by loving the community in sacrificial ways. We then also earn a voice to be heard. How do we care for the people in physical and spiritual poverty who we drive by on our way to the next church gathering? In what ways do we contribute to finding solutions within our communities? An integrated and intentional strategy moves us along the path to reaching our neighbors for Christ.

Without a doubt Christ-followers share a common calling to local ministry. Our goal is to be Christlike in our community. We want to create space where people encounter the living God and come to call on him as Lord and Savior. Sometimes that space opens in a grocery-store conversation, other times in a staff meeting at work. Wherever and whenever it comes, may we be more salt and light and less sawdust pickers and clanging noises (Matthew 7:3; 1 Corinthians 13:1).

GLOBAL OUTREACH

Before Jesus' local ministry began, he made an astronomical, crosscultural leap. He gave up his radiant, glorious home to embody God's message of grace and to pay the ultimate price for our eternal salvation. Jesus humbly obeyed the Father's call to go. He modeled what he would eventually call his followers to do: to take the good news into a fallen and broken world. The ends of the earth await this message.

I have talked with many people who question their individual roles as God's communicators. After all, the Bible records stories of God's encounters with people through dreams, visions, bonfires, and even a talking donkey. Why is *my* voice needed? He can no doubt repeat those means. Truly I can pray and fast for God to reveal himself through dreams and visions to the unreached people in the world. The Lord may indeed choose to reveal himself by miraculous channels, but his revelations are not within our control. Our part in the kingdom story does involve fasting and praying, but it also involves going and being actual, physical witnesses.

The theme of witness permeates the Scriptures: we who know God are called to share his message and be a blessing to all who do not yet know him. God called Abram out of his father's home and into a new land and promised that all peoples on earth would be blessed through him (Genesis 12:3). The prophets echoed the calling repeatedly to the nation of Israel. Isaiah, for example, relayed this message:

> "You are my witnesses," declares the LORD,
> "and my servant whom I have chosen." (Isaiah 43:10)

Jesus reaffirmed the calling as he told his disciples, "As the Father has sent me, I am sending you" (John 20:21). Therefore, we go to the ends of the earth.

The church has a clear mandate to tell the good news. Ed Stetzer expressed concern that "when the missional impulse is not expanded to include God's global mission, it results in believers moved only to minister in their own Jerusalem with no mind toward their Judaeas, Samarias, and uttermost parts of the earth (Acts 1:8)." God's expectation includes every nation, tribe, people, and language, but our human nature turns us inward. Without a crosscultural effort, we disobey Scripture.

A critical moment in global outreach came in 1974. The Congress for World Evangelization gathered missions leaders in Lausanne, Switzerland. Missionary Ralph Winter proposed a monumental shift in global missions strategy. He urged that "instead of targeting countries, mission agencies needed to target the thousands of *people groups* worldwide, over half of which have not been reached with the gospel message." This shift from people of the same country to people of the same ethnolinguistic group acknowledged the individuality and complexity of human existence throughout our planet. It infused a new enthusiasm as Christians grasped the potential for more effective evangelism.

Every country includes numerous people groups who share language, history, and traditions. Although estimates vary based on the definitions of ethnolinguistic groups, scholars agree that at least seven thousand groups remain untouched by the gospel message. Several thousand additional groups have fewer than a hundred Christians and no church to help evangelize their community. We have much to do among the unreached and unengaged peoples.

Global outreach can take different paths. As the Holy Spirit prompts, we discern where our gifts and abilities can best serve the needs of the nations. An informative resource for the journey is *Operation World*. Both the website and the handbook offer comprehensive profiles and prayer guides for all the nations. When exploring the possibilities, the church's strategy may include physical relocation, financial and in-kind support, digital delivery, or indigenous ministry.

First, our strategy may include physical relocation. The traditional use of the word *missionary* refers to a believer who physically moves to a new location to share the gospel message and establish a church among unreached peoples. It's understood as a long-term and evangelism-focused calling.

Among those called into global missionary service, some do indeed go where the name of Jesus is utterly unknown. Like the apostle Paul, their passion is to make the divine introduction: "It has always been my ambition to preach the gospel where Christ was not known" (Romans 15:20). The Holy Spirit drives them to people and places to till the soil and initiate the seed planting of the gospel message.

God calls others to dedicate their lives to the steadfast discipleship of new believers in Christ. Their ministry follows the model of Timothy, Priscilla, and Aquila. The early church relied on them and others with the same calling to teach the biblical precepts. Similarly, faithful missionaries today instruct, correct, and encourage countless new Christ-followers to mature in their faith.

The scope of missionary work has broadened over the years. Church planting is among the many ministry options. New ventures such as business as mission (BAM), for example, present promising alternatives. Missionaries who work through this model begin relationships through professional interactions. Business-minded Christians are teaching English and computer skills in all corners of the world. They meet physical needs before talking about faith. Innovators and entrepreneurs have introduced water-filtration systems, improved lightweight building materials, and solar-power lights. In many cases, the commercial endeavors also provide income to reduce the missionaries' personal fundraising needs.

In limited access countries, the BAM missionary will likely find a more receptive community than a traditional missionary seen as "competing" with local religious practices. Their work as an employee or an entrepreneur of a for-profit company serves local economic needs. Marketplace & Development Enterprises is one of the organizations leading the way for business as mission into countries closed to the gospel, as well as those requiring creative access for entry and ministry.

Being a Christian witness in the global economy offers incomparable opportunities to join God's mission to reach the ends of the earth. Eric King recently noted,

> In today's globalized economy, the doors of many unreached countries are closing to traditional Christian workers, but they are opening to professionals. Many global cities even offer generous benefit packages to attract Western expat talent. In God's amazing sovereign plan, abundant opportunities exist to go to unreached people and places around the world. Christian professionals are finding opportunities to take the jobs in which they excel and do them well, for the glory of God; and do them somewhere strategic, for the mission of God.

Every congregation needs to have a process to help its members explore the possibilities of a call into crosscultural missions. The responsibilities and liabilities are tremendous and not to be taken lightly. Consultations and preparation can be daunting and self-defeating before the process even begins. Mainline churches typically have a system in place through their denominational headquarters. A simple phone call or email can begin the discernment process. Churches and individuals seeking support outside denominational structures can partner with independent agencies, such as The Antioch Partners or Operation Mobilization. Some churches have also successfully developed their own missions-sending program.

An excellent place to explore this calling is at a missions conference. The massive gatherings of InterVarsity's Urbana and the New Wilmington Mission Conference, for example, offer opportunities to meet hundreds of people engaged in global missions. Church planters along with representatives of sending agencies, outreach organizations, and business-as-mission initiatives are available for conversation. Many missionaries' testimonies include life-shaping experiences at Urbana, New Wilmington, or other similar conferences.

Our strategy may also include financial and in-kind support. This includes monetary, prayerful, and tangible support for those who do physically relocate to the ends of the earth. Missionaries depend on various expressions of support from churches and individuals. Regular monthly contributions and one-time financial donations provide critical resources needed to be in the field. Gifts of time and material goods can also benefit the ministry and help to reduce some of the stresses in the field.

Across denominations most full-time missionaries now raise some, if not all, of their own financial support. The number of salaried, career missionaries continues to decrease. In 2015 the International Mission Board of the Southern Baptist Convention reduced their missionary staff positions by more than a thousand. Although raising support offers the opportunity to involve churches in global missions, the responsibility for the missionary can be overwhelming.

Our churches can help improve this process. Missionaries spend significant time on donor care. Newsletters, furlough visits, and emails

consume many hours—all in the interest of keeping individual supporters connected to their ministry. The demand for a constant social
media presence and appearances via Skype and FaceTime puts further
pressure on missionaries. Church leaders need to be sensitive to the
extent of these requests. We don't want to burden missionaries with ex-
cessive supporter care.

The local church can become more involved in global missions through
nonfinancial assistance as well. A congregant of a supporting church
could maintain a missionary's website or put together a monthly newsletter to update the missionary's supporters with stories and photos.
Snail-mail letters and gift packages to missionaries and their families offer
wonderful boosts of encouragement to those who can receive mail. We
can learn the birthdays and anniversaries of missionary partners and
honor them by recognizing their special days and flooding their email
inboxes and Facebook pages with messages of love and inspiration. We
can provide vehicles or temporary housing for missionaries home on furlough, or maybe even offer the use of a vacation home for a respite. One
ministry in the Midwest offers low-rent housing to missionaries seeking
to enroll at the local Bible college. Let's be creative in finding ways to bless
mission partners.

Media ministry is a third means of crosscultural engagement. A missionary's office may be in North Carolina, for example, but their ministry
is for people in Afghanistan. Radio waves and the internet are effective
tools for delivering the gospel message to isolated villages thousands of
miles away. Pay-as-you-go phones with internet access and short-wave
radios can reach even the most remote locations.

The emergence of digital technology has opened many doors to the unreached and least-reached peoples. Internet evangelism introduces the
gospel and offers avenues for Bible study and pastoral training. Media
ministry is the lifeblood of many Christ-followers who are unable to enjoy
a physical church gathering and the fellowship of other believers. For rural
churches, media provides access to a wealth of discipleship resources. With

an internet connection even the smallest church in the most remote location can bring great evangelists and teachers, such as Beth Moore and Max Lucado, to their events. People come to faith in Christ every day through the work of digital ministry.

The fourth path for global missional engagement by the Western church is through support of non-US missionaries serving in their native countries. Knowledge of the culture allows these indigenous workers to begin building relationships immediately. They skip the missteps caused by lack of familiarity with the language and culture. Despite enthusiasm and worthy goals, Western missionaries have unintentionally done harm in foreign locations.

Churches with a heart for the least-reached peoples may find indigenous ministry a way to fulfill their calling. Countries such as North Korea, Saudi Arabia, and Laos impose severe restrictions on or even forbid entrance of missionaries across their borders. Providing resources to the Christians already in the country may be the only way to support God's global mission in these locations. Furthermore, support for indigenous ministry extends the church mission budget. Financial expenses for a native Nepali pastor, for example, are lower than the funds required to settle a Western missionary in the Himalayan country. Language school, crosscultural training, and housing costs will always be higher for nonnative pastors.

The path to global disciple making has many possible starting points. We may be passionate about the spiritually lost, we may even love to travel, but the reason we go is to obey the divine mandate to take God's Word to every tongue, tribe, and nation. While we fully affirm the call to reach out to immediate neighbors, we cannot neglect the global call. A church strategy that does not include global outreach puts expectations of God and their congregants in a tiny box. The church's passion for local neighbors is laudable, but their lost connection to the global church is grievous. The mission remains unfulfilled.

FINDING OUR PLACE

The local-global conversation mattered enough to Jesus to include place names in his commission for kingdom work. He lists Jerusalem, Judea, Samaria, and the ends of the earth (Acts 1:8) in order to spread the gospel throughout the planet. Today we think about Jerusalem as the local mission field, Judea and Samaria as the national and regional fields, and the ends of the earth as the global field.

Whether discussing the church budget or considering the addition of a new mission partner, geography enters the conversation. Percentages fly around the room. Some church members envision a 50/50 split between local (which often includes national outreaches) and global mission. Other members want 90 percent of the missions budget dedicated to local outreaches with just 10 percent going to global mission. Yet another group articulates a well-crafted proposal for the majority of financial support to be dedicated to global outreach. Bitter battles play out as members advocate differing visions of the church's missions strategy.

But while committees debate the local-global divide, the world's population becomes increasingly more connected with one another. Craig Ott writes, "The ever-accelerating and intensifying phenomenon of globalization has been radically reshaping lifestyles and redefining our understandings of culture and ethnic identity." Ease of travel and increased access to technology have expanded our ability to connect across boundaries as never before in human history. Internet and satellite technology link suburban families in the United States with rural villages in Africa. Connections through Facebook, Twitter, and Skype defy political lines etched in cartographic history. International borders provide clarity for rule of law but radio waves and satellite signals travel in a world undefined by them. While country leaders seek the security of borders, crosscultural communications and relationships develop. Country boundaries become meaningless when friendships enter the conversation. The global village is now a reality.

In its purest geography, the kingdom of God embodies *boundarylessness*. Jack Welch, former CEO of General Electric, first coined this awkward term to "eliminate boundaries within an organization or a team and to create universal ownership of the organization's mission." The corporate world continues to apply the term to companies that break down barriers between departments and within their management structure. In the same way globalization is changing the nature of country borders, offering profound potential for evangelism.

Much of the local-global conversation in the church, however, seems unaware of the boundarylessness of globalization. Our lack of connectivity across the global church is a tremendous loss to the kingdom. The isolated efforts of individual congregations create a dissonance of loud gongs and clanging cymbals. Without listening to and engaging the Majority World churches—those in Africa, Asia, and Latin America—we are missing a growing and significant movement of the Holy Spirit. An international, interlinked scope of ministry would allow harmonious labor across the breadth of God's boundaryless kingdom.

Crosscultural relationships strengthen the church to be a more effective witness for Christ. Missiologist Stan Naussbaum writes, "Since boundary maintenance is a main preoccupation of all human groups, the existence of a boundary-transcending group is an anomaly. It will catch people by surprise, attract attention and demand an explanation. What is going on here? How is this possible? The explanation can only be Jesus, the Holy Spirit, and forgiveness, that is, the gospel." Places of plenty and places of want will always exist. I can't help but wonder how they may be part of God's plan to bring us into dependency on one another and, ultimately, on him.

How then can the church best respond to the local-global conversation? With globalization as a backdrop, we need to keep three specific factors in mind as we develop a missions strategy for the church: being global locally, partnering with indigenous missionaries, and contextualizing the gospel.

First, we can be global locally. With the movement of so many internationals into our communities for education and employment, our churches have the opportunity to reach out to non-Westerners within our own zip codes. Throughout the world, people of all nationalities now live side by side. According to Michael Gryboski,

> People are increasingly on the move, both voluntarily (for example, seeking better economic opportunities) and involuntarily (such as refugees fleeing conflict). In fact, the Center for the Study of Global Christianity estimates that 1 in 8 people globally live as part of a diaspora; this includes settled migrants who live outside their traditional homelands as well as current migrants.

The migratory flow of people offers new avenues for sharing the good news. Multicultural interactions have become the everyday norm for many people in our churches.

Pentecost presented the first multicultural opportunity for believers. As a major crossroads between the Roman Empire and the kingdoms of the East, Jerusalem brought together thousands of people of all nationalities. Some people were in town for religious reasons, some were residents, and still others were travelers just passing through. Miraculously filled with the Holy Spirit, Peter and the disciples emerged from hiding to proclaim the gospel message boldly. Visitors from Cappadocia, Egypt, Libya, Crete, and many other places heard the good news from these local Galileans. Many internationals came to faith in Christ and then took the message to their families who lived far beyond the city of Jerusalem.

Outreach among today's diaspora communities offers unprecedented opportunities to influence the ends of the earth from our own Jerusalems. Gryboski continues, "People in diaspora potentially are more open to a Christian witness than they might be in their homeland. In addition, people who might not have access to a Christian witness of any kind in their home areas are coming to places in which both international missionaries and local Christians can share with them." As internationals arrive in our communities, local ministry becomes global outreach.

A church northwest of Detroit, for example, wanted to reach out to the growing number of Japanese business people working in the automobile industry. As relationships formed, the US church developed a partnership with the Japanese Covenant Church in Japan. Together they planted a new church in the Detroit area and now have a traveling ministry to Japanese people across Michigan.

Opportunities are increasing for the Western church to serve immigrant populations. Whether corporate leaders or undocumented workers, immigrants' need for the gospel is the same. There are many ways to learn more about the ethnic composition in our communities. We can begin to grasp the diversity by studying US census results or through conversations with teachers at local schools. Discussions with the staff at the nearest refugee resettlement agency or the pastor of a church of an ethnicity different from our own can help us better understand our neighbors. Prospective kingdom residents are at our doorstep. We just need to meet them.

The second factor to consider is partnerships with same-culture missionaries. Although Western support is enabling many indigenous pastors to expand their reach, this strategy in isolation can become a stymied version of the Great Commission. Local outreach by an indigenous missionary is not a guarantee that all will hear the gospel message. As the authors of *Introducing World Missions* write, "It is often most difficult for those closest to a cultural or religious boundary to cross over it." Jesus himself struggled to share the gospel message in his hometown. Following his baptism and wilderness experience, he returned to Nazareth. In the synagogue of his childhood he read and applied the prophet Isaiah's words:

> The Spirit of the Lord is on me,
>> because he has anointed me
>> to proclaim good news to the poor.
> He has sent me to proclaim freedom for the prisoners
>> and recovery of sight for the blind,
> to set the oppressed free,
>> to proclaim the year of the Lord's favor. (Luke 4:18-19)

Instead of rejoicing in the fulfilled prophecy, Jesus' former neighbors drove him out of town.

Jesus tried once more to preach in his hometown (Matthew 13:55-58). Although amazed at his teaching, some were hostile. His longtime friends could not see past their familiarity with him to recognize the Son of God in their midst. Sometimes an outside voice is needed for people to hear the words. A foreigner can be a draw when people are curious about their culture and the message they bring. In a similar way, we host guest speakers in our US churches and promote them as an opportunity to invite new people.

Furthermore, the connection between a sending church and its cross-cultural missionary allows unique educational opportunities. The church in the West benefits in this exchange, learning about the needs and the joys of other customs, beliefs, and behaviors. Worldviews change. Cultural intelligence expands. The partnership becomes more about the relational and personal growth than the monetary support. The local church's missions strategy can never exclude God's call to send workers beyond its own country's borders. Otherwise we end up prioritizing geography over divine calling. The need for sending missionaries to foreign lands continues. The church's global efforts cannot be limited to money transfers.

The final factor to consider when developing a local-global strategy is effective contextualization of the gospel. Bruce Riley Ashford describes contextualization as the means to "effectively communicate the gospel to the people in a way they can hear and understand and apply to their lives." The cultural "flavor" of a new church ought to reflect the culture and context of the new believers, whether an isolated tribe in South America or an inner-city neighborhood in the United States.

Crosscultural interaction has long been a challenge for the church. In its formative years the differing lifestyle and rituals of the new Gentile believers caused disagreements among church leaders. Based on various outward standards, the early church questioned the veracity of the new believers' conversions. Long discourses in the New Testament, such as the passage on eating food sacrificed to idols (1 Corinthians 8:4-7), give instruction on grace-filled interactions. The apostle Paul taught church leaders to recognize and separate their Jewish heritage from their unifying kingdom citizenship.

As the gospel spread, the church needed to address cultural differences repeatedly. Eating habits, marriage rituals, and wardrobe vary with each culture that receives the good news, so the expression of Christian worship and lifestyle look different too. Is it okay to adapt the rhythmic drumming of a pagan ritual into a new song for the church? How does the minimal clothing of tribal people in tropical regions align with biblical precepts on modesty? Where does honoring the memory of family cross the line into ancestor worship? We continue to struggle with these questions today.

Our ability to navigate cultural differences enables us to be effective ambassadors for Christ. In our passion and haste to evangelize, we can unwittingly stamp our cultural practices onto the lives of new believers. Introduction of American dress and holiday traditions without regard for native culture has created a close—albeit unintended—affiliation of Christianity with the West. Missionary Brett Miller described a cab ride in a remote, non-Western location. The cab driver said he knew about Christians because of the "Church of Pants." Apparently, the Western missionaries had felt the men's traditional robes were inappropriate and encouraged new believers to wear pants. Lacking an understanding of the local community, they had damaged the culture as well as the local people's understanding of the gospel. Separating cultural norms from biblical standards is the first step on the journey to effective contextualization.

When we adopt the position of listeners and learners, we more accurately reflect the love and peace of God. The resulting humble awareness allows for appreciation of diverse expressions of human culture. Spiritual maturity about our cultural biases allows appropriate assessment, while also enabling us to reject nonbiblical practices such as human sacrifice and female circumcision. Leaving behind prejudices and speaking from biblical truths will bring the common ground needed for meaningful and practical ministry. When we can move out of egocentric thinking within our own church walls, we are able to join the Lord in his plan to restore all of creation. In obedience, we preach the gospel message to all who have not heard regardless of their physical address.

God's story is unfettered by space and time. We limit his expression of the good news when we allow location to cause us to value one people over another. Whether in the form of political boundaries or personal opinions, prejudices and hidden agendas can influence the church's missions strategy more than the biblical calling to go and tell the good news. Scriptural authority must prevail over our opinions about domestic poverty, national security, and all other relevant issues. The church's shared calling to be kingdom ambassadors motivates us to explore our differences and to align our passions into a united effort to serve neighbors near and far.

Our increasingly interconnected and interdependent world complicates the local-global conversation for the local church. As J. Rupert Morgan notes,

> The task of missions may involve crossing cultural boundaries, but it does not necessarily require crossing geographic and linguistic boundaries. Delineations between international and domestic missions can create false dichotomies that hamper the church in fulfilling its purpose in mission. The church needs to have a biblical, missional response to this change.

Geography cannot be the only criterion for missional engagement. It remains but one factor in establishing our churches' responses to serving the spiritually and physically vulnerable people in Jerusalem, Judea and Samaria, and the ends of the earth. Along with the many isolated and unreached people groups, restless hearts in post-Christian cultures hunger for the fulfillment that only the gospel can provide.

The boundarylessness of globalization highlights the freedom we have when developing a missions strategy. With discernment and maturity we can follow God's compass bearing anywhere, whether it directs us to neighbors next door or an ocean away.

QUESTIONS

1. Which one of the following scenarios best describes your place on the local-global continuum? Choose the one that most closely represents the direction of your calling. From your perspective, what makes your choice the best option?

❑ With growing concern for her community, Aya is passionate about the physical and spiritual needs of her immediate neighbors. She encourages her church to invest resources within their own zip code. She believes that as more believers invest time and money locally, less long-distance outreach requiring costly travel will be needed and more resources will be available for ministry.

❑ Brad desires to partner with agencies who serve within his region of the country. Brad feels convicted to help meet needs in places that are less than a day's drive from home. He believes that as churches connect within regions, the resulting networks can address a variety of needs without extraordinary travel expenses.

❑ Camila reaches out to international residents in her community. The increasing diversity represents nations from around the world, including places missionaries are not able to get visas to serve. She encourages her church to become more active with agencies who bridge the cultural differences and effectively share the gospel message.

❑ Dan chooses to partner with missionaries who serve beyond the borders of his own country. They reach across geographic, cultural, and linguistic barriers to connect with people who do not know Jesus. Dan and his church family support mission partners through financial donations, letters, and occasional visits.

❑ Eun Hae's concern for the most isolated communities draws her to missionaries and agencies who serve the THUMB (Tribal, Hindu, Unreligious, Muslim, Buddhist) people groups. They go into locations where people do not know—and may never have even heard of—Jesus Christ.

2. Rank the scenarios regarding your understanding of God's call for your church's missional engagement. Give examples to support your ranking.

3. How does increasing globalization impact your missional engagement? What influences does it have on your church's missions strategy?

4. What can we learn about the kingdom of God based on crosscultural experiences? What crosscultural outreach opportunities exist in your community?

3

CRISIS RESPONSE AND SUSTAINABLE DEVELOPMENT

Guilt. My heart accused me of being uncaring and judgmental. Again. I had rounded the city corner and a homeless man came into view. He was leaning back on the granite foundation of an office building. Within the next ten steps I decided to avert my eyes and pretend to be busy looking somewhere, anywhere other than down to my left where I was very aware of this vulnerable person on the sidewalk with a small tin cup and a sign that I did not read.

My previous visit to Washington, DC, ended with a different scenario but the same pangs of guilt. I had paused and put a few dollars in the up-turned hat of a disheveled man panhandling on a street corner. I walked away thinking I should have given a McDonald's gift card or a Ziploc homeless survival kit. What if he spends the money on alcohol or drugs? Why am I judging?

Even on the other side of the planet, I have wrestled with these emotions. Years ago I walked along a crowded Cairo street and a young girl approached me. Her timid smile and pleading eyes captured my heart. The sleeve of her tattered dress hung loosely as she held out her hand, palm open. I pulled a few Egyptian coins from my pocket and put them in her dusty, little hand. After a slight curtsy, she took off down the sidewalk. I glanced back with a smile only to see her laughing and giving the money to an older teenage boy, who joined in the laughter. I felt a different kind of guilt in this scenario, but it was a struggle nonetheless.

Should we give cash to people on the street? My friends tell me I am not alone in my struggles with how best to respond. My discomfort with these situations causes hasty reactions. I tell myself I will be prepared next time. But it's not so simple.

The Bible calls us to be generous and to give to those who have need. If the Lord prompts us to give money, a gift card, or hygiene kits, we ought to do so. The Bible doesn't say to give money only to those who have a productive plan for its use. Maybe the person experiencing homelessness needs money for medication. Or maybe he is a professional panhandler who will get up at the end of the day and walk to his car with the three hundred dollars he "earned" that day.

Is there another way?

Some years ago, when I was in New York City—and when I had a more flexible daily schedule—my friends and I invited a homeless man to join us for lunch. Over a burger and soda, we shared life stories. A hand on his shoulder and brief time of prayer brought joy and dignity into each of our lives. God created us to be in community, with one another and with God himself. The path of relationships leads to divine healing in hearts and souls, for individuals and communities alike.

We all develop views on the causes of poverty. These views contribute to how we respond. Is it personal failure or a broken system that keeps people in poverty? We generally have less tolerance for personal failures. Individual actions, however, do not transpire in a societal vacuum. Without knowing a person's full story, we are quick to judge and prescribe inadequate remedies.

The third of the seven conversations for discovering your compass bearing for missional engagement centers on response to the material needs of others. How can the church be more effective in serving a hurting world?

On one end of the continuum, the focus of missional engagement is emergency crisis relief. Survivors of hurricanes and earthquakes lose life's essentials: shelter, food, water, and livelihood. War and unrest create massive displaced people movements. Emergencies from medical crises to job loss also devastate families every day. Christ-followers passionate about relief mobilize to quickly respond to physical needs.

On the other end of the continuum, the focus of missional engagement is sustainability. When the moment of crisis has passed, long-term rehabilitation begins. Whether restoring services in a post-war community or walking with a felon in post-prison life, it is important to foster stability and dignity. With discernment and perseverance, development-minded believers commit to the slow process toward sustainability.

Where does your missional engagement compass point—toward crisis relief or sustainability or somewhere in between? In this chapter we will explore a wide range of crises encountered in this life, highlighting a variety of interventions and assistance people may require during these experiences. The church's response affects the victims as well as those observing from the sidelines. The ability to determine when to provide short-term relief and when to move into long-term development can challenge even the most well-equipped servant. Awareness of the full scope of our options will increase the effectiveness of our response.

CRISIS RESPONSE

The Bible has much to say about God's response to people in distress. Trapped in Egypt, "The Israelites groaned in their slavery and cried out. . . . God looked on the Israelites and was concerned about them" (Exodus 2:23, 25). Later Isaiah praised God for his compassion for the vulnerable:

> You have been a refuge for the poor,
>> a refuge for the needy in their distress,
> a shelter from the storm
>> and a shade from the heat. (Isaiah 25:4)

Over and over we read how God hears human cries (Psalm 34:6; 145:19; Jeremiah 33:3).

God's provisions were tangible and timely. In the book of Leviticus, for example, he made fruits and grains available to the materially poor. God's covenant with his people involved laws that mandated generosity. He made food available through their actions: "When you reap the harvest of your land, do not reap to the very edges of your field or gather the gleanings of your harvest. Do not go over your vineyard a second time or pick up the grapes that have fallen. Leave them for the poor and the foreigner. I am the LORD your God" (Leviticus 19:9-10). The first food pantries were on the edges of every field.

Jesus embodied divine compassion for those in need when he walked our land. He heard the pleas of Jairus as his sick daughter lay dying (Luke 8:40-56). He calmed the storm that filled the disciples with fear (Luke 8:22-25). He listened to the blind beggar's cry on the road to Jericho— "Jesus, Son of David, have mercy on me"—which has become a mantra for many believers today (Luke 18:38). We exhale these words when our own fail to form on our tongues. God's steadfast presence offers comfort no matter the chaos around us.

God sends us to be his representatives in the world. Caring for the needs of others remains part of that mandate. For "if anyone has material possessions and sees a brother or sister in need but has no pity on them, how can the love of God be in that person?" (1 John 3:17). We make our resources available—whether food, money, time, or talent—acknowledging that everything belongs to the Lord. We give generously to all whose paths we cross, not just loving "with words or speech but with actions and in truth" (1 John 3:18).

The crisis-response end of this continuum focuses on people in need of immediate assistance. Disasters—both natural and unnatural—create urgent circumstances desperate for relief. Assessments of food, water, shelter, and medical care prioritize the needs. We serve the victims while they are unable to care for themselves due to devastation from hurricanes, tornadoes, and earthquakes. In addition to the basic needs, affected areas often experience loss of electric power, damage to water and sewage systems, and destruction of bridges and roadways. Infrastructure problems compound relief efforts for the victims as well as the responders.

Churches outside a disaster area have much to offer. Financial and in-kind donations can ease the burden of immediate needs. In 2015 a massive earthquake wrought immense damage on the country of Nepal. Our church has a partnership with a Nepali church-planting ministry. I reached out to their leadership to ask how we could help. Funding was their biggest need. Their office in Kathmandu and the surrounding grounds had become an emergency shelter for survivors. In addition, pastors' homes, church buildings, and entire villages had been flattened by the earthquake. We shared the need with the congregation and received a special offering. Ten months after wiring the funds, our ministry partner emailed photos and accounting details of dozens of roofs and homes now repaired.

Church congregations can mobilize quickly to respond to needs. Before organizing a team to serve or taking a collection for clothing, however, we must research the needs. In our zeal to help, we can do more harm than good. Always ask how—and if—help is needed. Mountains of clothing and stuffed animals pour into crisis areas, unwanted and unusable. They become a secondary problem for the crisis responders.

When outside a disaster area, a few internet searches can produce numerous contacts to help identify needs. I have learned it is best to locate the disaster relief agencies that are involved and ask what kind of help is needed. When Hurricane Matthew brought massive flooding and damage to our neighboring state of North Carolina, I contacted the pastor of one of our denomination's churches in the affected area and asked how we could help: water, clean-up supplies, clothing, volunteers? The pastor and church leadership, however, were overwhelmed and spending long hours in crisis response mode. They struggled to articulate their needs and suggested I contact the North Carolina Disaster Information Center. Instead of adding to the burden of phone calls to the pastor, I should have called the center in the first place.

It's also never advisable to show up uninvited to a disaster area. Emergency response organizations have a name for unexpected arrivals: spontaneous unaffiliated volunteers (SUVs). A disaster site leader during the 2005 Hurricane Katrina recovery effort told me how they turned away numerous vanloads of SUVs. Volunteers arrived kindheartedly offering their unskilled labor. But expectations of housing and food stressed the already limited resources of the disaster response teams. Supplies are needed for the victims and first responders. SUVs have become such a problem that disaster relief organizations now have to train their workers how to deal with them.

Always contact the agencies who are taking the lead in a crisis. Faith-based organizations such as Salvation Army, World Renew, or Samaritan's Purse are likely to be involved. Secular agencies such as the Red Cross or the local Voluntary Organizations Active in Disasters (VOAD) may also be participating in relief efforts. Our response needs to be in line with recommendations from these first responders on the scene. Donations of volunteer hours and in-kind gifts may be welcomed. Both reduce costs for crisis relief agencies and local government services every day.

Equally intense are the smaller-scale disasters that strike individuals and families. Life and livelihood are also at risk in crises such as a cancer diagnosis, loss of a job, or death of a family member. Unnatural disaster crises can also be large-scale such as war, terrorist events, or famine. Their causes, while complicated, are mostly of human origin. In these cases, the international community mobilizes in the same way as responding to a natural disaster. Most relief agencies welcome involvement from the church and reach out with specific needs. We respond and stand as God's presence during the time of crisis. Once again, though, the key to being effective is to first ask what is needed.

Appropriate emergency resources can avert the deepening of a crisis. A family's home burned in our community. They had minimal insurance, but neighbors responded with temporary housing, clothing, and care during their rebuilding. A man in our congregation was unable to find employment after being laid off. It created tremendous financial stress on his family as the situation continued month after month. Our church's deacon fund provided help to bridge the gap until he began a new job. Crisis assistance brings much welcomed stability into an otherwise uncertain situation.

Poverty plays a key role in the advent of a crisis. A materially poor family is especially vulnerable in times of emergencies. Without a savings account or viable credit, a major car repair can become the trigger to unemployment. Their loss of transportation can remove the only means of getting to work. For someone without paid sick leave, an illness requiring hospitalization results in loss of income and the subsequent potential for the inability to pay rent. Homelessness looms. The crisis deepens.

The church steps in to help people halt their downward spiral. We respond financially to provide for immediate needs such as rent or medical bills. Christ-followers provide hot meals to homeless shelters, free car repairs, and Christmas gifts to impoverished children. Sometimes we do not know the people served by our generosity. Through our benevolence ministries or trusted mission partners, we willingly provide resources with no strings attached. Jesus did not say, "Feed my sheep, after approving their family budget," or "You clothed me, after I passed a drug test." The church's selfless generosity models God's amazing grace and sacrificial love.

But this is the point where the church struggles as well. There has been much discussion about the unintended harm of persistent free resources both locally and globally. At what point does crises relief end and unhealthy dependence begin? When emergency relief becomes the means of coping day to day and month to month, it prevents movement toward a sustainable life.

In their book *When Helping Hurts,* Steve Corbett and Brian Fikkert describe crisis relief as seldom, immediate, and temporary. They demonstrate the damage and the shame that chronic crisis-level services bring, especially to impoverished people. Although tension emerges with differing diagnoses of dependence, we nevertheless must become more attentive to identifying our role in the expanding problem. Robert Lupton points out that many of our well-intended efforts actually erode work ethic. Handouts of food and clothing undermine the dignity of the poor. Without a greater awareness of the potential for dependency, the church inadvertently becomes part of the problem.

Haiti exemplifies the crisis relief challenge on an international scale. Billions of benevolence dollars have come into Haiti and yet it is still the poorest country in the Western Hemisphere.

> For forty years we have been pouring masses of both public money and private money, mission trips, and charitable donations into that country, $8.3 billion up until this recent earthquake. For all that investment, Haitians are 25% poorer today than they were forty years ago when our charity began. What's wrong with that picture? What are we doing that's not developing people?

The answer: It's complicated.

Ultimately, we want our crisis response to undergird people for a brief time and help launch them into lasting transformation. The issues, however, are interrelated and complicated. Unemployment or underemployment, for example, keep people in crisis. Finding a job is difficult for someone with mobility restrictions, a criminal record, or mental health issues. And crises will repeatedly disrupt the lives of those with a minimal or nonexistent financial safety net.

We will always require a strategy for crisis response. First responders are necessary. Without firefighters, for example, our communities would be at great risk. No one would advocate closing the fire departments and merely adding more fire prevention curriculum to high school health classes. Stop-drop-and-roll instruction is not enough when the whole house is ablaze. Likewise, churches and relief agencies can work together to provide the most appropriate critical care for those in crisis. We need to be sure, however, that we are asking the right kinds of questions and taking measures that will produce lasting change.

SUSTAINABILITY

"Please don't build orphanages," the Zambian pastor pleaded with the American missionary. They hoped for something more than hundred-bed, impersonal institutions for the children.

"How then can we help?" It was 2003. The Lord had pressed the orphan crisis onto the heart of Gary Schneider. At the time, Gary had minimal knowledge of the HIV/AIDS pandemic or ways to help.

The beginnings of a partnership were forged that day in Lusaka. Caring for the growing number of orphans had become a draining responsibility for the Zambian church. Older members cared for numerous grand-children. Children of other extended family members now deceased also needed homes. And even more children abandoned to the streets gathered at the church doors.

As Gary and the pastor talked, an idea began to form. What if they could pair orphans with a widow to care for them? What if the children could be part of a new family where they could experience love and grace? What if the American church came alongside the Zambian church to add resources as needed for the widows and the new families? Every Orphan's Hope was born. Since then they have built and now sustain twelve homes bringing widows and orphans together for a new life and new hope in the future.

Both the Zambian and American staff will tell you that raising orphans is not an easy endeavor. Children arrive in their care having experienced much tragedy. Traumatic death of parents is often followed by unstable living arrangements. In some cases, the children have suffered physical and sexual abuse. They have had minimal schooling and may have numerous health issues.

With patience and perseverance, the widows gain the children's trust and a family develops. More than a decade has passed since the first mama and eight children moved into an Every Orphan's Hope home. The oldest children have since graduated high school. Several have earned college degrees—in law, journalism, and administration. Every Orphan's Hope continues to walk alongside these flourishing young adults. New children have moved into their beds and the families continue to grow.

Every Orphan's Hope demonstrates strategies of sustainability. The ministry is committed to the long-term care of children under their guardianship. Faith-filled widows who serve as house mamas provide necessary stability for growth. Donations from Zambian and US churches assist the ministry's funding needs. Financial resources also come from their business-as-mission enterprises—a bike shop and a poultry farm, which are increasingly profitable. The business-as-mission efforts also provide opportunities for the children interested in animal husbandry, bicycle mechanics, and marketing to learn and be involved.

On this end of the continuum, missional engagements prioritize sustainability and transformational development. In *Walking with the Poor,* Bryant Myers argues that the church can be a significant partner in this kind of engagement by attending to relationships with individuals, the community, and the environment. The prospect for sustainability increases when we journey alongside the people in need.

Our call to missions is a call to disciple people into transformed lives. Community is a critical part of this discipleship process. God created us to be in community, not only to care for one another but to teach and admonish as needed. As the Holy Spirit renews hearts and minds, our relationships with each other improve. People begin to thrive. A sustainable lifestyle emerges. Throughout Scripture, God gives well-rounded guidelines for living in community, including instructions about forgiveness, love, parenting, healthy interdependence, leadership, and justice.

During Jesus' three years of public ministry, he poured himself into his disciples. As they traveled together, Jesus mentored them. He taught through his encounters with people along the way as well as in private conversations apart from the crowds. Jesus was preparing the disciples to continue the gospel mission after his return to the Father. He modeled kingdom life, feeding them spiritual food so they would mature. The disciples became fishers of people and the foundation of what would become the living body of Christ, his church. Jesus formed them into a community that would be sustainable in upcoming times of crisis.

In today's missional engagement, similar mentoring continues to be the most effective tool for transformation. As Natasha Sistrunk Robinson explains, mentoring is "a trusted partnership where people share wisdom that fosters spiritual growth and leads to transformation, as mentors and disciples grow in their love of Christ, knowledge of self, and love of others." Relationships are foundational. The opportunity to teach and the willingness to learn create the best place for growth. The most sustainable ministries include intentional mentoring in their development strategies.

The lack of relationship between servers and recipients of aid opens the possibility for harm. Despite our well-intended desire to respond to needs, we can misread circumstances due to our lack of knowledge and lack of contact with those who can speak honestly about the conditions. Corbett and Fikkert note that "the biggest mistakes that North American churches make—by far—are in applying relief in situations in which rehabilitation or development is the appropriate intervention." Charitable handouts can create an unhealthy dependency instead of helping an impoverished family move toward personal accountability and sustainability.

A family in desperate need of groceries arrived at our church. We had a small food pantry converted from an unused Sunday school classroom. We helped them choose food and received a shy smile from their blond, curly-haired toddler. We waved goodbye, grateful to be able to help. We learned later, however, that this same family had turned up at a church two miles down the road with the same story of crisis job loss and medical bills earlier in the week. And another church the week before that. They had been making the rounds through the churches, receiving generous handouts everywhere they went. It became apparent that food-pantry shopping was their purposeful means for feeding their family.

If our church would have had a sustainability strategy in place, we would have learned more about this family's situation to determine the nature of their crisis and how best to help them. Without such a strategy, however, we likely contributed to their prolonged life on the margins. As a result of this experience, our area churches began discussing how to better serve our community and formed a new ministry, in partnership across denominations, to better assess requests and to meet needs responsibly.

The church is uniquely positioned to work within all realms of the community. Members have a wide range of abilities and knowledge to contribute. When willing to take on the hard discussions of need with truth and love, the church can mobilize for far-reaching influence. Congregation members who serve as mentors, English language teachers, or elementary school tutors develop relationships that will affect lives well into the future. Churches work with long-term projects such as microloans, job-readiness programs, financial education, and health clinics that bring profound transformation within communities.

The place to start sustainability ministry is to evaluate the needs and the resources in the area we are called to serve. Meetings with government officials, service providers, and school counselors will help us form a picture of overall trends. Conversations with community members in all socioeconomic groups help us to fill out the picture. International Justice Mission offers a free workbook for congregations to explore the complex issues of violence and injustice, and to identify resources, strengths, and gaps in services in their communities. The tool suggests ways to collaborate and helps identify partners for next steps in both national and international settings.

The community review at my church revealed a gap in services to help unemployed and underemployed people step into sustainable work.

Through additional research, the Jobs for Life ministry came to our attention. Prayer and conversation with partners who serve the impoverished, at-risk population affirmed the value of a job-readiness program in our area. Jobs for Life offered a faith-based curriculum that focused on the dignity of work, overcoming personal roadblocks, and preparing vocational plans. A key component of Jobs for Life is the support and training of mentors for every student. Seven students graduated from our first class.

Pastor and entrepreneur Kurt Vickman had a vision to bring healthy and affordable food into his community. In the summer of 2015, he founded the co-op Good Grocer in Minneapolis. Members of the co-op volunteer two and a half hours a month. With over three hundred members, the reduced personnel costs allow the nonprofit store to pass substantial savings onto members. Although anyone can shop at the store, customers who are members receive a 25 percent discount. Vickman, an advocate for helping people preserve dignity in poverty, notes that "sometimes we forget that even people who are struggling financially or in other areas of their lives still have a desire to give back and to be a part of something that is having an impact on people's lives. We have to stop treating those in need as helpless clients and start to see them as gifted contributors."

World Vision is one of the global ministries committed to the long-term goal of overcoming poverty while being mindful of appropriate crisis care. They provide disaster relief as well as assistance toward community development. Amid all the outreach projects, their Christ-centered focus remains at the heart of every decision. One of their warehouse facilities is located in impoverished Philippi, West Virginia. The small yet dedicated World Vision staff responds to emergency needs, but the bulk of their time is spent developing relationships. Partner coordinator Kris Wamsley spends her days connecting people and churches for community-led initiatives, such as mentoring programs and resourcing educators to improve the lives of children. Their home-repair program offers a hand up for local families while also providing service opportunities for out-of-town churches wanting a meaningful short-term mission project.

Sustainability-focused missional engagement has a very different timeline than crisis-relief outreach. Economic development takes time to come to fruition. Corbett and Fikkert observe that "the North American need for speed undermines the slow process needed for lasting and effective long-run development." Instead of focusing on the beginning and ending of a program, sustainability celebrates incremental steps along the process: A young man earned his driver's license. Rejoice! A family moved out of a shelter into a home. Praise God! We recognize the slow, steady progress of the journey together. Continued healthy community interactions allow the strength and value of relationships to positively influence the situation.

The spiritual component of faith-based development organizations separates them from their secular counterparts. As Christ-followers, we believe the ultimate healing of a life is found through restoration of relationship with Jesus Christ. Even when surrounded by overwhelming physical needs, we seek to fulfill our role as witnesses of the kingdom. We need to introduce the gospel message into the story at some point in the recovery process. If every person on the planet attains sustainability yet lacks Jesus, we have not fulfilled the Great Commission. Creating space for reconciliation and restoration with God and others brings the miraculous transformation toward life abundant.

FINDING OUR PLACE

No situation exemplifies the crisis response–sustainability dilemma quite so starkly as whether we should give cash to a person experiencing homelessness. It's complicated and there are numerous factors to consider. Before our next encounter with a person or outreach in need, we must determine our place on the continuum.

Churches committed to sustainability can find goal setting challenging. Ministry on this end of the continuum is unpredictable and more susceptible to failure. Success is measured in the progress of those served rather than the number of congregants involved. Furthermore, fundraising campaigns for development efforts struggle to gain the momentum that crisis relief receives. As Corbett and Fikkert observed, "'We fed a thousand people today' sounds better to donors than 'We hung out and developed relationships with a dozen people today.'" In crisis-response initiatives, items collected and distributed might indeed meet the needs of men, women, and children, but those who contribute usually are not able to develop relationships with the recipients.

How then does the church fit into this complex conversation? As the body of Christ, we are more than distributors of goods and services. Although the next high-efficiency solar panel and the newest distribution model for emergency food rations may hold great promise, the church's primary purpose for the world is to become the unwavering, tireless, steadfast presence of God's grace and love. In his book *To Change the World*, James Davison Hunter defined the concept of faithful presence as the guiding standard for our work. He described the mission as "a theology of engagement in and with the world around us." As we travel this life, God is fully present within us. In turn, we learn to be fully present with God, with one another, and to our tasks. Ministry emerges out of these unwavering, tireless relationships, not from the pressing demands of the physical needs around us.

Throughout human history, God models faithful presence. He sought Abraham and promised engagement: "I will establish my covenant as an everlasting covenant between me and you and your descendants after you for the generations to come, to be your God and the God of your descendants" (Genesis 17:7). To the nation of Israel, he reaffirmed his presence: "Then I will dwell among the Israelites and be their God" (Exodus 29:45). The Old Testament records God's repeated affirmations of his faithful presence to his people.

Then, in the ultimate sacrifice, God gave Jesus as his gift of presence. "The Word became flesh and made his dwelling among us" (John 1:14). He continues his steadfast presence through the filling of the Holy Spirit, who is Christ in us (Colossians 1:27). We, the church, then unite as one to represent God himself. "In him you too are being built together to become a dwelling in which God lives by his Spirit" (Ephesians 2:22).

We bear the responsibility to be present, to re-present the kingdom to the world. We are Christ's faithful presence in crisis situations and in long-term development efforts. The difference between grace and harm lies in the state of our presence. If my underlying motivation for giving cash to a homeless person is to assuage guilt, I am not living into faithful presence. I'm silencing my emotions. Likewise, if solving world hunger becomes the core of my ambition, engagement in the world narrows to personal objectives rather than attending to God's mission. If my goal, however, is to be attentive to God and his promptings, I then meet needs in a much different attitude of presence. Obedience to God's work then drives ministry.

In his book *Faithful Presence*, David Fitch offers practical application for Hunter's concept. From presence reconciliation to gospel proclamation, Fitch's disciplines equip the church to experience God then prayerfully step into mission with him. The focus is on relationships. Fitch explains, "The best thing we can do is be present. Tend to what God is doing. Tend to the presence of our Lord in this place." We discern our mission through faithfulness in our relationship with God and with others.

When faithful presence guides our crisis-sustainability compass bearing, the gospel message enters the story with ease. Fitch reminds us that in order to share the good news of Christ, we need to be present first. "Presence precedes proclamation." Already attentive to God, we are sensitive to the Holy Spirit and his gentle promptings. Throughout the crisis-sustainability continuum, our journey's goal continues as "a call to be sure we do our development with an attitude that prays and yearns for people to know Jesus Christ."

A church's missional engagement can effectively emerge anywhere along the continuum. What does God's faithful presence in your church's missional engagement look like in your community? A one-size-fits-all strategy does not exist. Geography, people, and circumstances are unique.

"God finds someone or a people and sends them to a place as an entry point." Sometimes he prompts to give a cup of cold water. Sometimes he prompts a Nineveh-like transformation of entire cities. Sustainable humanitarian work would no doubt have been appreciated in Nineveh, but that was not God's petition to Jonah. Sometimes God gives cooking oil for the next day and only the next day; sometimes, though, he fills barns to overflowing.

Consider your current missions efforts. Do they primarily focus on crisis relief? If so, maybe the Lord is calling you to serve as an emergency care provider in your community. Our willingness to open doors and wallets to people regardless of the hour or the inconvenience is his faithful presence to those in need. Financial and in-kind donations allow many food pantries, homeless shelters, and faith-based disaster relief agencies to keep their doors open. Consider new ways to support the staff and volunteers of the ministries who will be Christ's faithful presence with people in the places where you and I cannot go.

Perhaps the Lord is prompting your missional engagement more toward sustainability. Through discernment, you can begin making steps to balance crisis response with development efforts. Start with small steps. One church provided weekend food for children in a low-income elementary school. Members then helped with a summer reading program. Their faithful presence in the school built trust to then be invited to come weekly to mentor children. Corbett and Fikkert remind us that "the goal is not to produce houses or other material goals but to pursue a process of walking with the materially poor so that they are better stewards of their lives and communities, including their own material needs."

Before committing to increased work on the sustainability end of the continuum, we need the full support of the church leadership. It is a marathon. Compassion fatigue, physical weariness, and setbacks can discourage even the most motivated congregation. A leadership committed to development will help congregants stay the course. Our desire is to follow God's promptings and to be his presence in the world, even when completion may be years away.

Wherever the Lord leads, our desire is for people to notice God at work. As Peter responded to the crowds following healing of the crippled man in Jerusalem, "Why do you stare? . . . It was God!" (Acts 3:12-13, my paraphrase), so too we want to participate in miraculous restorations and then say the same: "Don't look at us. It's all God!" We want people to stare in astonishment at things that only God could do. All glory and honor are his alone.

QUESTIONS

1. Which one of the following scenarios best describes your place on the crisis response–sustainability continuum? Choose the one that most closely represents the direction of your calling. From your perspective, what makes your choice the best option?

   ❏ Aaron works alongside organizations who provide emergency relief for those in disaster situations. He serves as the point person for his church's response to the urgent needs of victims of natural disasters (including earthquakes, hurricanes, floods, and forest fires) and displaced persons due to war, unrest, and famine.

   ❏ Byung Moon's heart lies with impoverished people in his community who struggle with daily needs. He willingly gives his hours every week to cook at the local homeless shelter, deliver food to shut-ins, and help raise money for urgent rent or utilities-assistance requests.

   ❏ Caroline serves with a ministry that responds to crisis needs but also provides personal consultations with assistance recipients. She believes an immediate response to emergencies alongside follow-up guidelines will bring the most compassionate and responsible means to impact her community.

   ❏ Deandra prefers to give her time and financial donations to ministries that prioritize accountability with crisis assistance recipients. She helped set up measurable standards at the food pantry, for example, by requiring that clients enroll in a budget class after their third month of seeking food assistance.

❑ Ervin partners with ministries focused on sustainability. No funding or staff time is spent on crisis response. With discernment and perseverance, he and his church are development minded and committed to the slow journey toward sustainability.

2. Rank the scenarios regarding your church's response in the crisis response–sustainability conversation. Which ones most mirror your congregants' actions? Give examples to support your ranking.

3. How do your church's goals in this continuum align with the work of your mission partners? How can you be more involved with those most closely corresponding with your call?

4. What factors impact your decisions in meeting the physical needs of others? Is anything missing in your evaluation of ways to serve those in crisis?

5. What changes would you recommend for prayerful consideration in your church?

4

TIME AND MONEY

Our church staff visited the Renwick Gallery in Washington, DC, recently. A branch of the Smithsonian Institute, it displays three-dimensional art in its most innovative forms. Hanging from the central staircase is Leo Villareal's lighting sculpture. Embedded in 320 vertical, stainless steel rods are thousands of tiny LED lights synchronized in a mesmerizing dance, courtesy of a customized computer program. In another room, the museum's featured exhibit that month focused on June Schwarcz's works. Her enameled pieces dazzled with their metallic hues of blues and purples. On the second floor, decorative ceramics and textile crafts from various artisans waited patiently for us to pause and ponder their meaning. Reflection and conversation emerged as we strolled through the gallery.

At the base of each artistic piece, a name plate displayed the title, artist's name, date of the work, and the donor. Generous patrons made the displays in this public place possible. Sometimes several names followed the "gift of" declaration. The larger exhibits also included foundations and endowments as benefactors.

People who value the arts and have the financial means donate great sums of money for the advancement of visual, performing, and literary creations.

Because most artists are not self-supporting, donors' gifts can also extend to the artisans themselves. The funds allow art to thrive where it would otherwise never be birthed into expression. Donors play a significant role in encouraging people to be involved, both as spectators and participants.

What is needed more: talent or money? Without the artist obviously we have no art. Without food, however, we have no artist. The world of art needs supporters as much as it needs artists. Gifted people create inspired works, then in partnership with art enthusiasts cultural influence expands. We appreciate artists and patrons through recognition at banquets, in playbills, and on nameplates in art galleries. They both steward critical contributions to bring art to audiences around the world.

A similar question exists in the world of missions. What is needed more: time or money? The fourth of the seven missional engagement conversations revolves around the expression of stewardship. The continuum ranges from gifts of time on one end to gifts of money on the other. Effective missional engagement needs both resources. Fundamental understanding of the biblical principles of giving will allow wise choices throughout the continuum. We also need to allow for movement along this continuum as our capacity to give fluctuates within the ebb and flow of life.

On one end of the continuum, the focus is tangible investment in the kingdom. It's the donation of assets to trusted ministries and organizations. In addition to money, offerings can include items of value such as clothing or even a vehicle. Not only do gifts benefit the recipient, they are good for the giver's soul. Scripture repeatedly calls us to hold loosely to our possessions and to be good stewards for their ready use. Christ-followers at this end of the spectrum willingly give the shirts off their backs or write sizable checks as needs arise.

On the other end of the continuum, the focus is the giving of time and talents. All believers receive spiritual gifts for strengthening and encouragement in this life's journey. Some receive a salary for their talents, but voluntary contributions by teachers, preachers, administrators, and helpers are the heartbeat of the church and her ministries. Time cannot be multiplied, compounded, or borrowed. Its donation extends this priceless gift otherwise unavailable. As we mature in our faith, we become more willing to trust the Lord with our time. Never anxious about tomorrow's needs today, our flexibility with plans and agenda demonstrates our faith in the Lord.

Where does your missional engagement compass point: toward tangible financial investment or toward the gift of time? The kingdom of God needs the full scope of resources to bring the good news to those who do not yet know Jesus. The church's faithful stewardship cares for and makes available this plethora of assets for the benefit of all people.

As we make our way through this conversation, consider the possibilities in your life and the wider membership of your church. Some opportunities present themselves immediately, while others may be for future life stages. The availability of a parent differs from someone without dependents, as do the options for a recent college graduate versus an empty-nester. Resist judging the capacities of others on this continuum. Paths open and close for expressions of gifts and time as circumstances change. We will examine benefits and hazards at both ends and look for the Spirit's guidance to make wise choices.

DONATING MONEY

My husband and I bought our house in 1994. Over the years we've painted the bedrooms, remodeled the kitchen, replaced the roof (twice actually, thanks to two damaging hail storms), and landscaped the front yard. We have invested thousands of dollars in our home. I am grateful to also have a car, a graduate school degree, and a retirement plan.

Actually, though, none of this is mine. Not one bit.

Everything belongs to God. This is the fundamental basis for this missional engagement conversation: "The earth is the Lord's, and everything in it" (Psalm 24:1). God is the source of everything, including our clothes, cars, furniture, and bank accounts. Furthermore, as the Creator of life, he is also the source of our talents and abilities. Everything comes together for his use and his blessings. "For from him and through him and for him are all things" (Romans 11:36).

This biblical understanding alters my perspective.

So let me try again: God blessed me and my husband with a house in 1994. Over the years we have painted, remodeled, re-roofed, and landscaped with income earned through abilities that the Lord gave us. In an overflow of grace, we also received cars, advanced education, and extra funds to prepare for emergencies and retirement. We are abundantly blessed.

My responsibility with these gifts is to steward them well. To be the steward of an estate is to manage the owner's property. In the hands of capable stewards, provisions are put to use and they flourish. In the same way, we are managers of God's resources. My husband and I willingly loan and give away possessions. We financially support several ministries out of the blessings of our income. We strive to be faithful stewards of God's gifts.

Jesus' final teachings focused on the kingdom standard for stewardship. First, he told a parable about a manager preparing to go on a journey (Matthew 25:14-30). The man entrusted money to each servant, then left for an extended period of time. When he returned, he rewarded the two servants who had used and multiplied the money. The third servant, who was fearful of using the manager's funds, had done nothing with the money. He had protectively hoarded the money, then returned it. Due to his laziness and lack of resourcefulness, the manager tossed him out of the household.

Jesus followed this parable with a story about sheep and goats (Matthew 25:31-46). In the last days, he will separate people as a shepherd separates sheep from goats. The sheep represent those who have been generous with their wealth and their possessions. They provide for the most vulnerable in their midst. They will receive eternal reward for their righteous actions with God's provisions. The stinginess of the people represented by the goats prevent their participation in God's future kingdom.

Our role as Christ's followers includes the call to generosity. The early church first modeled benevolent giving when a famine spread throughout the Mediterranean region. Believers gave as they were able, then Barnabas and Saul brought the donations to those in need (Acts 11:27-30). Later the church in Macedonia and Achaia gave money to the poor in Jerusalem (Romans 15:26). God continues to prompt and enable his people to respond to needs near and far. "You will be enriched in every way so that you can be generous on every occasion, and . . . your generosity will result in thanksgiving to God" (2 Corinthians 9:11).

The trouble comes when we hesitate to use provisions when called on to do so. Our self-centered nature drives spending on personal desires. We build vast savings accounts to expend on ourselves later. We become protectors instead of stewards. We are heavily invested in the protection of our own lifestyle, comfort, and future. How much do we really need to save for the proverbial rainy day? Our over-attachment to God's gifts has led to increased hoarding of kingdom resources.

Temperature-controlled storage units are popping up across the country. In 2016 annual self-storage revenue in the United States was estimated to be about 36 billion dollars. It's expected to continue growing at an annual rate of 3.5 percent. The national average cost per unit is $87.15 per month. That means many of us are paying over a thousand dollars a year to store stuff we never use. Imagine how much could be used to meet the needs of others.

Responsible stewardship of resources enables us to be active participants in God's global mission. When we place our trust in God rather than in the stuff he gives, we are able to see and respond to the needs around us. When we have a kingdom mentality for our money and possessions, we will be ready to use these resources for the Lord's purposes, which include our own enjoyment: "Command those who are rich in this present world not to be arrogant nor to put their hope in wealth, which is so uncertain, but to put their hope in God, who richly provides us with everything for our enjoyment. Command them to do good, to be rich in good deeds, and to be generous and willing to share" (1 Timothy 6:17-18).

Speaking the good news is free but the preacher needs sustenance and shelter. As the expression of art expands with the generosity of philanthropists, the reach of missions increases with financial support from the body of Christ. As we shift our mindset from ownership to stewardship our ability to release financial and material resources increases. Churches and individuals answer God's promptings in different ways. The variety of needs and our unique abilities to respond require ongoing discernment in each situation.

Time and time again I have witnessed how the Lord provides. Within my church divine prompting brought a car for a needy family, emergency plane tickets for a missionary, and dental surgery for an uninsured young adult. "God is able to bless you abundantly, so that in all things at all times, having all that you need, you will abound in every good work" (2 Corinthians 9:8). God intends us to be without need. As the early church first came together, they shared resources and "there were no needy persons among them" (Acts 4:34). Our wealth is for his kingdom use.

The Holy Spirit inspires missionaries to use their unique gifts and passions to share Christ in all corners of the world. We, the larger body of Christ, have the responsibility to come alongside them to enable their mission. There are many kinds of ministries in need of financial support, including those focused on developing and revitalizing churches, supporting and equipping missionaries, and offering professional services.

One of the most direct ways to contribute to the spread of the kingdom is through donating to new church developments. God calls missionaries to places where unreached or unengaged peoples live. Some serve where the name of Jesus is unknown; others serve in places where revitalization of the church is needed, such as in Europe. You may be a one-time provider of seed money to begin a new effort, or the Lord may be calling you to an ongoing effort with a longer-term commitment.

Sister-church partnerships present another avenue for church growth. For example, St. Giles Presbyterian Church in Richmond, Virginia, partners with El Talbiya Evangelical Church of Giza, Egypt. Their relationship includes more than financial giving. Medical clinics, pastoral support, and prayer commitment are encouraging a revitalization of El Talbiya and an improved understanding of Arab culture among the people at St. Giles.

Organizations dedicated to equipping missionaries rely on the support of churches and benevolent givers. These ministries include agencies, such as The Antioch Partners and IDEAS, that help people discern their missions call and prepare them to serve. They also provide missionary care in the field, including accountability and counseling as needed. Some ministries provide respite locations for missionaries and their families when taking sabbaticals or pursuing continuing education.

Additional equipping organizations advance God's global mission by responding to specific needs on the mission field. Wycliffe, for example, translates the Bible into native languages. Child Evangelism Fellowship provides evangelism curriculum in child-friendly formats. Ministries such as Barnabas Aid, International Christian Concern, Open Doors, and Voice of the Martyrs serve believers in nations where the church is persecuted. Equippers come alongside God's servants to enable their ministry in the field.

Faith-based agencies dedicated to bringing justice and humanitarian care to the poor offer additional ways to connect with God's work globally. Because their work is pro bono, their needs for financial support are ongoing. International Justice Mission works to end slavery and to give voice to the most vulnerable men, women, and children. Attorneys, investigators, and government employees come together to improve due process throughout a nation's justice system. Christian Legal Aid hosts clinics and provides civil legal assistance in the United States to people unable to afford representation through traditional means.

God is also calling his people to relieve suffering and pain in other humanitarian sectors. Medical missions, such as MAP International, are bringing health and healing to thousands every year. Orphan-care organizations, such as Compassion International, Every Orphan's Hope, and World Vision, change young lives every day. Crisis pregnancy centers, homeless shelters, and food pantries provide valuable services in local communities. Disaster relief agencies, as discussed in the previous chapter, provide emergency services in places where you and I cannot go. Funding for professional personnel and relief supplies is in constant demand.

Increased awareness of the potential harm of charitable handouts has given rise to several financial planning organizations. Through innovative savings and credit programs, they are helping people step into economic sustainability. World Vision's Savings for Life initiative, for example, provides a reliable banking option for impoverished people to prepare for emergencies and to grow a business. Operation Blessing International's microloans combine lending platforms with small-scale enterprises. Within the United States, programs like Individual Development Accounts empower people toward responsible financial practices. Women and men are stepping out of poverty through their participation. As talk-show host Trevor Noah noted, "People love to say, 'Give a man a fish, and he'll eat for a day. Teach a man to fish, and he'll eat for a lifetime.' What they don't say is, 'And it would be nice if you gave him a fishing rod.'" Skills are important, but without tools, the lessons remain in the classroom. The church can provide the resources for improved chances of success.

Tension mounts in missions giving when we attempt to define efficiency and effectiveness. Metrics and statistics remain a difficult topic within Christian ministries. Is the three thousand dollars spent on an evangelistic rally worth the souls of forty-two teenagers who came to faith in Christ? Were the twelve hundred pounds of green beans, rice, and cereal from last month's food drive worth the staff's time to organize and transport the donation? Business standards fall short when applied to eternal goals and matters of the heart. We can, however, align expenses and income with our missions strategies. With a clearer picture of our missional engagement goals, we are better equipped to analyze the effectiveness of donations.

Church leaders are responsible for researching the financial health of potential partners. We can read annual financial reviews and make the results available for others to review also. We can find out whether the ministries are accredited by the Evangelical Council of Financial Accountability (ECFA) or a comparable institution and whether they have responsible and sustainable goals. Then, as our partnerships continue, we can review these ministries regularly.

A final word on the practice of directed gifting. When a donation is given for a specific purpose, the receiving agency must abide by the requests of the donor. A family made a generous donation, for example, to a church in memory of their grandfather. The gift was designated for the purchase of a folding machine for the preparation of the Sunday morning bulletins. The church staff, however, did not need a folding machine. An awkward conversation followed between the church administrator (not wanting to be ungrateful) and the family (wanting to honor their grandfather who had taken copious sermon notes on the bulletin every week). The donor had the right to request the donation be returned but instead allowed it to be used for another purpose. Before putting parameters on a gift, please talk with the ministry about their needs.

Our call to stewardship is clear. We are caretakers of the many gifts given by God. Whether financial or material possessions, we must act responsibly with their use. In this life's journey, Paul instructs, "See that you also excel in this grace of giving" (2 Corinthians 8:7). Generosity demonstrates our understanding of this biblical mandate.

GIVING TIME

"All our needs are taken care of by our paid staff. We do not need volunteers," said no church or missions leader ever. It's not a flaw in our business model. It reflects God's plan for his people.

Because we are formed in the image of God, his creativity is built into our nature. "For we are His workmanship, created in Christ Jesus for good works, which God prepared beforehand that we should walk in them" (Ephesians 2:10 NKJV). We want a meaningful life, which for most of us includes hands-on experiences. In a CNBC survey, 55 percent of millennials found more value in giving time than donating money. Seniors (aged sixty-five and up) expressed equal desire to give money and time.

While slightly less than the younger generation, retired adults still yearn for purpose. It is not in our nature to be merely a cash-giving people.

God created each of us with abilities for such a time that he chooses. He expects us then to use these talents willingly for the benefit of others. "Each of you should use whatever gift you have received to serve others, as faithful stewards of God's grace in its various forms" (1 Peter 4:10). Profound selflessness and deep concern for others characterize the purest use of gifts and talents, serving not for personal recognition but to honor God. No effort is wasted no matter how small or seemingly insignificant. "Whatever you do, work at it with all your heart, as working for the Lord" (Colossians 3:23). We give our very best during the hours we serve.

When we ask for *volunteers* to help with the next church event or ministry, we misspeak. The request expresses the worldly need for an unpaid worker to do a job. It's a casual request: "If you have spare time in the coming week, would you be able to show up?" Author Michelle van Loon notes that "calling members of the body of Christ 'volunteers' communicates a 100-calorie snack-pack version of the all-encompassing call to discipleship Jesus described." It misses the significance of family connection and expectation.

The Hebrew and Greek words translated as "volunteer" in the Bible convey a more sacrificial tone than the contemporary English sense of merely an unpaid worker. Old Testament writers used *nadab*. It expressed a person's willingness to give freely, such as a lengthy time of service (Nehemiah 11:2) or for war (Judges 5:2, 9). In the New Testament, the term is *hekōn*. In 1 Corinthians 9:17, for example, Paul referred to voluntary preaching of God's word. He gave willingly and freely to the people in Corinth. Similarly, we offer the gift of ourselves to serve others.

This is where the church's role becomes vital. As Gary Hoag, Scott Rodin, and Wesley Willmer explain, mobilizing people is one of the marks of a Christ-centered ministry. Leaders "acknowledge that the Holy Spirit is the power of ministry, so they help Christ-followers discern their giftedness.

This positions the members of Christ's body to use their gifts to bless one another." The church bears responsibility to help people connect their gift-edness, interests, and talents with the needs in the community and beyond. Increasing awareness of the needs enables church leaders to connect congregants to people and places to serve.

People willing to commit unpaid time over a lengthy time period are truly more precious than gold to churches and ministries. A few conversations can help find the right ministry fit for someone.

First, explore their God-given interests and passions. Do they spend personal resources to feed the hungry in their community? Do they spend hours praying for people who have not been reached with the gospel message? Discovering these passions will enable Christ-followers to connect their servant heartbeat with kingdom needs. For instance, Katie, who loves children, began helping with a church's outreach to an impoverished local elementary school. First, she helped with a summer reading program for the children, then she started serving weekly during the school year as a tutor, and eventually she began helping with the Good News Club at the school. Her love for the Lord manifests itself in her passion for the children.

Second, take an inventory of spiritual gifts and abilities, which can help people narrow their focus. Spiritual gifts inventories are available from numerous sources in both online and paper forms. We each have other abilities as well—such as with computers, music, or athletics—that can be offered to the Lord's service. A computer expert can redesign a ministry website. Musicians can lead choirs in underserved schools. Sports-loving Christians can coach teams. The administrative gifts of retired teachers can bless ministry offices with improved order and organization. Undergirded with prayer, all these offerings can become a platform to share the gospel in word and deed. When congregants' abilities are matched with the needs of ministries, lasting partnerships develop.

Third, discuss time availability. When talking with missionaries and mission partners, be attentive to the variety of ways your church family could help—often there are weekly responsibilities as well as periodic ones. Some people have hours to give each week, others have less time. Commitments with work and family affect availability. Developing projects for completion at home may allow more people to serve. When hosting a food drive at church, for example, equip families to run a parallel food drive in their neighborhood, classroom, or workplace. Another example is the "giving tree" we set up in our church lobby every December, where we hang hundreds of simple construction-paper ornaments with requests from our mission partners printed on them. For the homeless shelter, for example, these requests include travel-size lotions, ten-dollar grocery store gift cards, and wool socks. Not only do congregants take ornaments and shop for the donations, but they are involved in the initial set-up of the giving tree. Moms with toddlers, families wanting to do a project together, and retired seniors have all helped to make the ornaments over the years.

As we shepherd congregants to serve, it is vital we maintain ongoing support and healthy boundaries. I have encountered too many believers who feel unappreciated and overlooked amid the hours they donate. Burnout is a real threat for unpaid kingdom workers. Church leaders need to avoid creating a selfless-volunteer-for-Jesus model that is guilt driven and exhausting. People graciously give their time, but they also appreciate having a voice in the ministries, receiving training, being able to change responsibilities, and even taking time off.

God uniquely equips each person called into our church families. He "has placed the parts in the body, every one of them, just as he wanted them to be" (1 Corinthians 12:18). The gifts exist to build up and enable growth in the body of Christ. "From him the whole body, joined and held together by every supporting ligament, grows and builds itself up in love, as each part does its work" (Ephesians 4:16). When someone is not serving, a part is missing! It's like a family gathering for a holiday dinner and there's no main course because Aunt Freda did not come. Her contribution is dearly missed.

As the body of Christ working together, we willingly give our time and talents to the collective kingdom work. The musician who leads the praise band, the family who bakes meals for new moms, and the plumber who repairs leaks for free contribute with extravagant gifts to God's mission. Hearts soften and the gospel goes forth:

> If you spend yourselves in behalf of the hungry
>> and satisfy the needs of the oppressed,
> then your light will rise in the darkness,
>> and your night will become like the noonday. (Isaiah 58:10)

Shine on.

FINDING OUR PLACE

What is needed most—time or money? Our understanding of effective use of resources has a profound influence on missional engagement. We evaluate potential partners and ask if giving time or donating money most benefits the kingdom. Although this question arises frequently, we are actually approaching the issue from the wrong perspective.

Both time and money can be used for good or evil. They can be tools for God's use in this life. He already is the owner and operator of everything on earth. Time itself belongs to him. He set the hours in motion when he created the sun and the moon.

The real question lies in what we do with the tools. Our use of time and money reveals our core motives. It's the physical manifestation of faith. Sacrificial giving, whether of time or money, acknowledges our dependence and right relationship with the almighty God. He desires our complete devotion. It's not the number of hours we give or the number of zeroes on the bank check that advances the kingdom message, though both do indeed benefit the spread of the gospel message. Instead of keeping a tally sheet, however, God rewards us for the condition of our hearts.

The perfect model of service is our Lord Jesus. He gave up being in God's presence to become a lowly tradesman from a small rural village. He walked among us not as royalty to be served but as a humble messenger and ultimately the sacrificial offering for humanity. Jesus described his mission—and ours—as "whoever wants to become great among you must be your servant, and whoever wants to be first must be slave of all. For even the Son of Man did not come to be served, but to serve, and to give his life as a ransom for many" (Mark 10:43-45). As Christ's ambassadors, we share in this active and participatory calling.

The essence of this time-money missional engagement conversation is generosity. When we hold loosely to possessions—physical items, time, and money—we are able to freely give them away. This openhanded living is made possible when we are confident that the Lord will meet all our needs. In our Western culture such trust can be a daunting challenge. God alone is the giver of all things, yet we revere self-reliance, multitasking skills, and the stock market.

We need to recognize the talents, money, and time we have received are not ours alone. From food and clothing (Matthew 6:32-33) to wisdom itself (James 1:5), God gives in abundance. When we in turn give of them sacrificially, we demonstrate our gratitude to and dependence on God. He is Jehovah-Jireh, our ample and benevolent provider (Genesis 22:14). Stewardship of these gifts includes use along with responsible guardianship. "This service that you perform is not only supplying the needs of the Lord's people but is also overflowing in many expressions of thanks to God" (2 Corinthians 9:12).

Without a doubt, every mission and outreach ministry would benefit from more resources. They are rarely self-supporting. As we seek to improve and increase missional engagement, both the church and benevolent givers would gain from a review of their time and money use. An assessment could reveal unnecessary spending, inefficient time use, and even wasteful practices.

The simple principle of spending less in order to give more could release tremendous financial resources for kingdom use. In the words of Forrest Gump: "Momma said there's only so much fortune a man really needs, and the rest is just for showing off." In a similar spirit, Tony Campolo once asked, "Would Jesus drive a BMW?" Do we really need seven-thousand-square-foot homes? Is a forty-million-dollar building necessary for a church's new worship center?

Lessons in time management could also release significant resources for God's use. For example, can we improve efficiency of committee meetings? When lay leaders exhaust all their available hours in church meetings, precious little time is left to serve the community. What of the hours we spend browsing social media, binging on favorite Netflix shows, and playing never-ending video games? Better use of personal time will reduce the wasted hours ticking off the clock. Relationships will grow as we spend time with one another rather than rushing off to the next appointment squeezed into our schedule.

As the church teaches biblical principles of stewardship, support for missional engagement increases. Newfound time and money become available as we better understand godly generosity. Trust in God's faithful presence will influence use of our divinely loaned resources.

With sheepishness in his voice, one pastor told me, "We're a check-writing church." His apologetic comment came out as we brainstormed ways to help his aging congregation engage more with missions.

"Well, that's the place to start!" I was genuinely excited.

"Yes, but they don't want to *do* anything."

"But they are doing something," I told him. "They are giving their money. Your congregation is mostly senior citizens, living on fixed incomes. Celebrate their generosity."

"I don't know," he said, looking down. "Our annual report lists all our missionaries, but we're not really involved in their work."

"What about sharing news from the field? I'm sure your missionaries' websites and newsletters have lots of testimonies and stories. Share them with your people! As your congregation becomes more familiar with your missionaries, those connections will develop."

"How?"

So many examples came rushing to mind. I told him about a church that learned about children in a rural orphanage who got soaked as they walked to school during the rainy season. The church raised money and bought dozens of rain ponchos. I told him about another church that learned that their mission partner dreamed of building a new center for people experiencing homelessness. A new space could expand their ability to serve the most vulnerable people in the community. The ministry wanted to include space for social services, classrooms, and a free medical clinic. The church joined the fundraising efforts. A by-product of both efforts was increased awareness of each ministry's work. Additional congregation members connected with them and were now also giving hours in service.

Many missionaries and outreach agencies offer creative ways to connect with their ministry. Child sponsorship programs bring money and people's time together; letter writing, gift giving, and occasional visits cultivate relationships that benefit both the recipient and the donor. Specific project backing—such as building a school, funding a clean water well, or providing a cow for an impoverished family—allows donors to feel more personally involved in a ministry's work.

Some ministries sponsor special events to combine time and money. World Vision's 30-Hour Famine has raised millions of dollars while also challenging teens to thirty hours of fasting and increased awareness of global hunger. In the summer of 2014, the ice bucket challenge took over social media. Although ridiculed by many people, it raised over 115 million dollars for ALS research (also known as Lou Gehrig's Disease). We suffer marathons, hike mountains, and bike across states in searing summer heat to benefit specific ministries and causes. This experiential approach to support raising continues to expand. Interestingly, research suggests that our "willingness to contribute to a charitable or collective cause increases when the contribution process is expected to be painful and effortful rather than easy and enjoyable."

Who can answer the question about whether time or money is needed most? Both are essential, and both require contributions from the larger body of believers. Members in every church sacrificially give time and money. Some members among us have jobs that result in abundant financial resources. Their monetary gifts enable kingdom growth through humanitarian purchases, facility rent, and staff salaries. Others give more out of their time. Their talents and abilities bring countless donated hours of professional expertise and willing hands into missional engagement. Maybe it's our obsession with the bottom line, but we tend to value large financial gifts more than abundant gifts of time. It is shortsighted to declare one end of the continuum more important than the other. The poor widow who gave two small copper coins offered a picture of utter dependence on the Lord. Out of her poverty we see her total investment in God's kingdom. As we trust the Lord, we will be able to follow the Holy Spirit's promptings with our resources.

What if Christians were more generous toward global needs? Richard Stearns writes,

> Imagine how stunning it would be to the watching world for American Christians to give so generously that it: brought an end to world hunger; solved the clean water crisis; provided access to drugs and medical care for the millions suffering from AIDS, malaria, and tuberculosis; virtually eliminated the more than 26,000 daily child deaths, guaranteed education for all the world's children; provided a safety net for the world's tens of millions of orphans. Think what a statement it would make if American Christian citizens stepped up and gave more than all the governments of the world combined because they took Jesus seriously when He said to love our neighbors as ourselves.

Imagine the profound effect we could have by contributing hours, sharing knowledge, and donating necessary funding. The church has not always given time and money well. But what if we started now?

QUESTIONS

1. Which one of the following scenarios best describes your place on the time-money continuum? Choose the one that most closely represents the direction of your calling. From your perspective, what makes your choice the best option?

❏ Alice's financial generosity overflows. Her primary missional engagement is tangible investment—whether financial or material—for kingdom use. She willingly gives clothing and food and writes sizable checks as needs arise.

❏ Basim prefers to support ministries through financial or in-kind donations along with occasional hands-on service. His church's local mission partners, for example, welcome people to assist with office needs, and their international partners host short-term teams.

❏ Seeking balance in missional engagement, Cindy encourages her church to include a 50/50 blend of serving opportunities and financial support. She strives to have the same balance in her own commitment to missions. She spends many afternoons at an after-school program working with at-risk teens, while also being a monthly financial donor for the ministry's expenses.

❏ Damien is committed to serving partner organizations with regular hands-on help. He willingly gives of himself, being flexible with hours and not being anxious about tomorrow's needs today. Occasionally he donates money to help with the ministries' financial needs as special requests arise.

❏ The focus for Emma's contributions is the gift of time and abilities. She believes the utilization of gifts and talents plays an important role in the relational connections between churches, missionaries, and those in need.

2. Rank the scenarios regarding your church's expression of stewardship. Which ones best reflect the responses of your congregation? Give examples to support your ranking.

3. How do your church's goals in the time-money continuum align with the work of your mission partners? In what ways can you increase involvement with those most closely corresponding with your call?

4. In what ways could you increase generosity in your life? How could your church create an environment that values generosity throughout the time-money continuum?

5

BENEFITS AND DRAWBACKS OF SHORT-TERM TEAMS

I n 2013 I led a short-term mission team to serve with a ministry partner in inner-city Pittsburgh. Among their outreach efforts, they hosted coffee houses for people who were drug-addicted and without a home.

While setting up to serve lemonade and Italian ice, I felt the Spirit's prompting to talk with Josh, one of the staff members. I walked over and struck up a conversation. I learned he worked on the staff because he had once been homeless and this ministry had changed his life.

I asked him what helped him get off the streets.

"This place." Josh pointed down to the gravel of the vacant lot where we stood.

A holy pause passed between us as we glanced around the lot now brimming with impoverished guests and our mission team.

"How did you overcome your addictions?" I asked.

"When homeless, I came here nearly every week. One of the leaders told me my problem was not the drugs and alcohol. It was a lack of something in my life . . . God. First time I ever heard that. It was why all the rehab had failed me."

Awed by his honesty, I listened intently to his story. "It was the mission teams like your students here. They showed me this Jesus and his unconditional love. They smiled and talked and served and cleaned up. They prayed. Their love broke through my heart."

"How long have you been off the street?" I asked.

"Seven years."

My heart skipped a beat. I did the math. "Our student ministry served here in Pittsburgh that summer. Here in this very coffee house."

"I was thinking actually that you look familiar. I think you served me." Josh smiled and joy washed over his face.

Sometimes the Lord lifts the veil to reveal the results of kingdom labor. We must wait until heaven to truly comprehend all of his purposes and his works. Occasionally, though, he allows us the privilege of seeing the fruit on this side of glory! We never know the impact one day or one week will make. Sometimes it's an eternal, life-saving difference. Our week in Pittsburgh became more than a short-term project. It was a living classroom. It affirmed the value of mission teams.

Sadly, however, I also have experience with short-term missions that are more like a dysfunctional, chaotic circus. Teams arrive unprepared and untrained. One group arrived at a disaster relief site expecting a trip to the mall to get work shoes (really!). Agencies that host are not always prepared before the team arrives. One place we served had received our money but forgot to order building supplies. Another location had broken pipes and no toilets at our housing. One port-a-potty arrived by day's end for thirty of us to share. Benefits for the community paled in comparison to the time and money spent for the team. With deep regret I admit I have served on teams that may have done more harm than good.

Debate about short-term mission projects rages on. It is the subject of the fifth of the seven conversations for discovering your compass bearing for missional engagement. Most scholars believe the short-term missions trend will continue to build momentum. Books, seminars, and webinars address ways to tame the rising deluge of teams who serve ineffectively.

The short-term mission conversation includes advocates of short-term experiences as well as those who outright reject the practice. The church's position in this conversation affects the church budget, spiritual formation strategies, and relationship with ministry partners.

Short-term mission projects are crosscultural travel for ministry purposes. They can be weekend experiences or longer commitments. Numerous factors contribute to the mixed reputation of short-term mission projects. This chapter examines their strengths and weaknesses in order to explore the church's role in this global phenomenon.

On one end of the continuum are those who believe that short-term mission teams can effectively work alongside a missionary or mission organization to multiply their ministry in the community, for example by hosting a children's outreach, working on a home repair project, or teaching a women's seminar. These close partnerships can yield beautiful results through mutual encouragement and the movement of the Spirit. Our definition of the church broadens exponentially when the body of Christ embraces best practices for short-term mission projects.

On the other end of the continuum are voices that denounce short-term mission teams. Stories of ill-prepared teams, painted-and-repainted concrete walls, and damaged community relationships document the tragedies of short-term mission teams. Third-party organizations offer short-term mission trip experiences but lack relationships within communities. Troubling outcomes leave more problems than they solve. Critics argue that short-term mission participants are merely searching for a vacation with a purpose rather than serving to support needs on the mission field. They advise that the extravagant fees paid for such Christian tourism would be better spent on support for career missionaries.

This chapter provides a framework to explore your theology of short-term projects. Are short-term missions an expression of the Great

Commission? Do they play an effective role in the spiritual formation of participants? Can they enhance relationships with ministry partners? Or are they simply tourism? Churches need to wrestle with the concerns about short-term mission experiences as they develop their overall missions strategies.

BENEFITS OF SHORT-TERM MISSIONS

The afternoon sun warmed the hut. I paused to allow my colleague to translate my English teaching into the Karen dialect of the Thai village. The women and men in the room leaned in to hear the words in their native tongue. A few nods and guttural affirmations encouraged me that the message was transferred.

Outside the window opening, peeping chicks drew my attention as they scurried behind their strutting mother hen. A cow and her calf moseyed by the open doorway. Barefoot and dusty children darted in and out of the hut. All eyes returned to me. I continued my teaching on women leaders in the Bible. Then another pause for the translator. Repeat.

Earlier in the day, I had watched a young man emerge from the jungle bush. With a well-worn Bible in one hand and small bedroll in the other, he had walked several days to attend the teachings. He was a pastor in a village farther south. In a bamboo hut down the dirt path, my missions teammate and home church pastor was teaching the basics of preaching.

I looked around my sparse classroom and marveled at my presence in that place at that time. Our ministry in Thailand came after years of partnership with a career missionary. My heart swelled with joy at God's grace to draw me to this unreached and forgotten corner of the planet. Here the Lord would use us to teach the Scripture to his followers so young in their faith.

Our small team of six came to Thailand at the invitation of our longtime mission partners, Austin and Sinte House. Along with the indigenous staff of Farthest Corners, the Houses' focus is in Southeast Asia, specifically

Burma/Myanmar. Our short-term mission group came to teach pastors, women, and children. Farthest Corners evangelizes and disciples emerging leaders among the nationals. Occasionally they host short-term missionaries to bring special training, much like we host guest speakers in our US churches.

Our team's time in rural Thailand improved our understanding of Farthest Corners' mission field. We stayed with local families in their stilt homes, sleeping on bamboo floors and eating traditional foods. As we immersed ourselves in the culture, we learned about differing worldviews and the unique struggles of the Asian church. Furthermore, we deepened our connection with our mission partner. Many miles of traveling and teaching together enriched friendships that would last well beyond the two weeks we were there.

When we turn to Scripture, we find evidence to support short-term mission projects. On numerous occasions, God incorporated short-term assignments to fulfill his kingdom purposes. Nehemiah's fifty-two-day project to rebuild the walls in Jerusalem may have been the first short-term mission construction project. God's travel plans for Jonah directed him on a brief evangelistic mission to an enemy nation. Paul's missionary travels were a series of short-term missions in different cities. The Lord guided him on seed-planting ministry from city to city throughout the Mediterranean region. Most places Paul arrived and departed within weeks, sometimes within days.

Concern over the financial costs of short-term missions prevent many people and churches from undertaking the effort. Scripture, however, reminds us that God is the ultimate owner of all our wealth. Sometimes he directs its use in ways beyond our understanding. From the opulent temple in Jerusalem to the expensive perfume that anointed Jesus, we observe how the Lord's use can differ from our expectations. I would likely have echoed the disciples' objection that "this perfume could have been sold at a high price and the money given to the poor" (Matthew 26:9). But we have an extravagant God who works in extraordinary ways.

No price can be placed on affection. God places unparalleled value on relationships. Financial resources alone mean precious little in our journey to fulfill the commandments to love him and to love one another. As orphan care advocate Gary Schneider once told me, "God sent Jesus, not the gold of Fort Knox." It was the physical presence of Jesus and the relationship he offered that changed the world. Similarly, the Lord calls us to be present with others. No amount of worldly wealth will replace people caring for one another. The influence of a Christ-filled heart cannot be duplicated through cash.

There are numerous benefits that can be derived from short-term missions. First of all, these teams can enhance partnerships between the local church and mission partners. Furlough visits begin relationships, but the connection strengthens when short-term mission teams serve in the field. As missiologist J. Rupert Morgan explains, "The twenty-first-century North American church does not want to be involved in missions simply by proxy but wants an active role, and short-term mission trips fulfill this desire." Congregations want to connect beyond financial support and monthly updates from the field. With ease of travel and the means to do so, members are ready and willing to serve.

A congregation can also learn more about the culture and the missionary as the team is training for their short-term mission project. Sunday announcements, newsletters, and blog posts can update the church and share needs from the mission field. A financial collection can be organized to purchase items in the field, such as supplies for the children's ministry, household goods for orphanages, or a night out for the missionary family. Not only will the donation be an economic blessing to the missionary's community, it also offers a way for the congregation to be involved. Team leaders can also share a calendar of the team's expected daily ministries, which not only invites the congregation to pray specifically but also gives them the chance to learn more about the missionaries' daily life and ministry.

Short-term missions also increase our appreciation of globalization. The reality of our multicultural life is evident today in our neighborhoods, workplaces, and the marketplace. Short-term mission projects develop our cultural intelligence by increasing awareness of other people and their customs. David Livermore explains that short-term missions "can enhance our ability to interact across cultures day in and day out as we move throughout the twenty-first century world."

When serving with the Thailand short-term mission team, for example, I confronted my culturally limited view of the gospel. The guilt-innocence culture of my Western worldview caused me to understand the salvific work of Jesus differently than people do in Asian cultures. In their shame-honor worldview, the language of redemption and "payment for sin" is not effective when sharing the gospel message. I learned instead to describe God's desire to restore honor by removing the shame of sin. Jesus' life, death, and resurrection allow my disgraced self to enter God's family. God's kingdom spreads more effectively as we become more educated ambassadors of his message. Lessons learned for a short-term mission project alter our perspectives for a lifetime.

Short-term missions blast the sides off the carefully constructed boxes of our faith. Altered forever is our understanding of God's attributes and human nature when we experience life on the mission field. Through miraculous provision and sacrificial community, I have observed aspects of God I rarely noticed at home. Team members and I experienced his presence when he healed a young girl in Africa, provided extra nails to complete a roofing project, and started up a broken truck despite a severed fuel line. When the doubts and difficulties of life roll in, I remember the tangible lessons God taught us on the mission field.

Following Hurricane Katrina in 2005, Jenny and Aaron Gordon served as missionaries with Forward Edge International in New Orleans. They worked with over two hundred teams to help rebuild the community. Repeatedly, they heard how the Lord had uniquely touched team members during their short-term mission experience. Jenny noted,

Many people said it was one of the first times they had been on a mission trip or used their vacation time to do something for God. They felt compelled to come by the tragedy but only really discovered God's hand in the midst once they exited their normal life. Spending time with others in travel, working side-by-side, doing devotionals on-site, and hearing the stories of the homeowners slowed them down from their fast-paced lives to realize that God has a plan for this world. The questions they began to ask themselves sparked a desire to understand God in a way they may not have needed to previously. Over and over again, as people left to go home, many said they realized that God had a plan for the world *and* their life. They wanted to return home being more intentional about figuring out the plan and getting to know their God more deeply. This had profound and lasting effects on these individuals as well as their churches. We saw this in the repeat teams serving in New Orleans. The changed lives people had seen in their fellow congregants inspired them to come and seek God in a similar way. Praise God for short-term mission opportunities that provide a space for people's hearts and eyes to be softened and opened to God's plan for the world *and* his plan for each individual believer!

When exploring the possibilities for short-term mission projects, begin with conversations with your church's mission partners. Ongoing relationships with missionaries allow support churches to match their gifts and abilities with the needs on the mission field. Ask if and how a team might be helpful for their ministry. As you explore options, listen carefully and honestly evaluate if your potential team would truly be able to meet their needs.

Another option is to work with well-established ministry organizations. You will serve in their neighborhoods with their ongoing outreaches. Ministries such as the Bowery Mission in New York City, Jesus People in Chicago, and the Pittsburgh Project in Pennsylvania provide opportunities for churches to experience the daily life of serving the poor. You might also know a church in a crosscultural location that would welcome a team to help for a special outreach. Connect with them directly to discuss the possibilities.

An option that many churches pursue is to work with a short-term mission agency. They connect churches with projects around the world. Choose an agency that invests in long-term development in the communities they serve. Most short-term mission agencies provide an experienced facilitator, training materials, and debriefing suggestions for post-trip discussions. Their expertise is especially valuable for churches just stepping into short-term mission projects. You can narrow your search as you define parameters for your short-term mission. Some agencies specialize in a geographic region or in a type of project, such as home repair or evangelism. Some organizations, such as Son Servants, Group, and Center for Student Missions, bring multiple churches together for a larger group experience, while others, such as Forward Edge International, organize custom trips.

Well-done, short-term missions remove us from day-to-day routines to serve God's kingdom beyond the comfort zone of home. We are filled with wonder and awe at God's hand as we experience the sights, sounds, and possibilities in every new place. We discover the diversity and creativity of the church across many cultures. Effective short-term mission projects are much more than tourist visits as they involve the church in crosscultural ministry that's making a difference in the kingdom.

DRAWBACKS OF SHORT-TERM MISSIONS

The first short-term mission teams I led served our church's mission partner in rural New York. For several consecutive years we loaded fifteen-passenger vans with teens, adults, and supplies to come alongside some aging congregations to help with vacation Bible school and home repair. I am forever indebted to our church members with construction skills who came with us to oversee roof work, drywalling, and siding projects.

During the preparation for the projects, I spoke frequently with the New York churches. They matched the skills of our team with the repair projects.

They sent copies of their vacation Bible school curriculum, so we could plan themed games and relevant opening skits. I also received information about the church kitchens, allowing us to plan meals and pack needed supplies, including large pots, griddles, and cleaning materials. Much work went into supporting summer activities with our ministry partner up north.

Then I discovered the world of professional short-term mission team agencies. As a busy youth director, the ease of working with one point of contact drew me like a moth to a candle. The agency handled the job sites, housing, and training packets. Glorious!

The first few short-term mission trips with the agency went well. They did the work of connecting with local churches and missionaries. I did the work of preparing the team. Our closest relationships, however, became the short-term mission agency and not the people on the mission field. The shift away from the mission-field focus began to trouble me. Things came to a head with our short-term mission trip to a Midwestern city. Everything bad I had ever heard about short-term missions happened on this project.

The problem started when our vans pulled up to the church. Our hosting church expected a team half our size. Space for sleeping bags was limited. Additional food shopping would require extra work throughout the week from their small congregation.

We had prepared for two children's camps. Early Monday morning we showed up at both sites with supplies and smiles, ready to begin. Neither location knew we were coming. The soup kitchen where we expected to serve breakfast the next two days turned our team away. They too did not know to expect us and were already fully staffed.

Then I learned our agency facilitator had never been to this city. When he arrived (the same day our team drove in), he was weary from leading a ten-day trip in Mexico. The business of short-term mission trips was grinding on.

Through God's grace, our team's work gradually took shape. Our students and adults worked together with the host church and work sites.

New plans evolved. Children heard the gospel message. New friendships formed.

During this trip, however, the short-term mission agency and our team caused great harm. We burdened our work sites with unexpected children's programming. Facility openings and closings, as well as additional custodial hours, impacted their staffs. Follow-up with the children after our departure was doubtful. We put the soup kitchen staff in an awkward position. And we overwhelmed a well-intentioned host church and left them exhausted by the end of the week.

I had become the problem my missionary friends lamented. Never again.

Short-term mission agencies have become big business. Their original intent provided churches with two clear benefits. First, they offered expertise in project organization and community knowledge. Second, they saved time for church staff members by taking on the tasks of communication and logistics. The church could subcontract the short-term missions administrative and preparatory work to professionals.

With the increasing ease of short-term mission projects and the growing demand for experiential learning, the number of trips exploded. Agencies worked with church leaders they met at student ministry conferences or through websites and mass-mail flyers. They multiplied their efforts to find new ministry partners in the field. The lack of relationships with churches and partners, however, began to create problems. Church groups arrived unprepared. Field partners neglected to add projects to their calendars. The divide between the teams and their hosts deepened. The potential for the connected global church got lost in the logistics.

Even more than the disconnect in the mission field, the increasing financial investment in short-term teams (STM) has led many church leaders to question or even prohibit short-term mission projects. Airfare, housing, and food add up to tremendous costs for churches and participants alike. Is this the best expense of kingdom resources? Corbett and Fikkert offer this example:

> A highly respected organization equips and manages national evangelists across the continent of Africa. The total cost of these evangelists is $1,540 per year for salary ($1,200), mountain bike ($250), and backpack, team shirt, and bedroll ($90). . . . Contrast these numbers with the expense of doing an STM trip. Spending $20,000 to $40,000 for ten to twenty people to be on location for two weeks or less is not uncommon. The money spent on a single STM team for a one- to two-week experience would be sufficient to support more than a dozen far more effective indigenous workers *for an entire year.*

The cost of every short-term team needs to be evaluated. What is the purpose of the team and does it support the vision of the church and the mission partners? Especially troubling, writes Rupert Morgan, is when "churches include STMs in their annual budgets in response to the growing participation by youth groups and church members, leaving less money for career missions. Budget restraints result in career missionaries now raising more support from individuals than from churches." In the current climate of decreasing financial donations to the local church, the leadership is giving extra scrutiny to every expenditure.

An unintended consequence of the short-term mission industry is its now prominent position in the spiritual and emotional growth of teenagers. Brian Howell explains,

> Throughout the decade of the 1970s, these trips were becoming a means for relatively affluent U.S. Americans to expose their kids (or themselves) to mission work. They were opportunities to gain spiritual insight through experiencing the simple faith of the poor, encountering non-Christian/non-evangelized communities firsthand while enduring a taste of the hardships of living outside of the United States.

Short-term mission experiences have almost achieved rite-of-passage status in the church and in the community.

I recall the conversation like it was yesterday. I was greeting students as they arrived for our Sunday evening gathering. A young man I did not know came through the front entrance.

"Hello, I'm Tyler. My friend Paul goes here."

"Hi, Tyler! I'm Sharon." I held the door as he came in. "Paul is in the kitchen helping get sodas and food. I'm glad you're here. We're beginning a new discussion series."

"Yeah, Paul told me." Tyler glanced around as more students arrived. "He also told me your church does mission trips."

"We do. Are you interested in missions?"

"Sort of. But also, my school counselor told me to find a church doing a mission trip this summer. She said it would look good on my college application."

Tyler mistook my speechlessness as affirmation. He continued, "Can I get the details about it tonight?"

This scenario repeated itself numerous times over the following years. The public schools had discovered the potential of short-term mission projects. The church, mine included, welcomed the new students onto our mission teams.

The short-term mission environment provided an effective means to introduce teens not only to missions but also to faith in Jesus. Conflicts arose, however, when teams arrived with mixed motives. Youth leaders focused on the meaningful experience for participants derailed plans prepared by hosting missionaries. An ice cream break for team bonding disrespects community members prepared to work. Evening debriefs lasting to midnight result in exhausted and short-tempered team members on the job sites the next day.

Groups traveling primarily to expose participants to crosscultural experiences view poverty strictly as lack of material wealth. They benevolently give gifts of candy, clothing, and trinkets out of their abundance. In doing so, however, they harm themselves with an increasing pride and harm those they had hoped to serve by decreasing their dignity. They leave more damage than benefit in their wake. Short-term mission participants who serve from a posture of privilege miss many blessings from mature believers in the materially poor places of the world. The economic dichotomy overshadows the spiritual and emotional wealth ready to be shared.

Many reasons exist for us to reevaluate the purpose of short-term missions. When our teams create more work for field missionaries and ministries, we need to examine whether the benefits are worth the expenditures. We might better care for our mission partners in their ongoing work through prayer support and increased financial and in-kind donations as needed.

FINDING OUR PLACE

Vast territory lies between the two ends of this chapter's continuum. Advocates for and against short-term missions raise compelling cases for their positions. At the heart of the conversation is the global communion of Christ-followers. As brothers and sisters in the family of God, we want to connect with one another. We want to visit, bring a meal, and pass along hand-me-down clothes like a large extended family. The way we visit demonstrates the worth we place on one another and on the community built among us.

When my husband and I took an anniversary trip a few years ago, I asked my parents to stay with our children. I fully trusted Mom and Dad to care for them and manage their elementary-school activities. Because my dad can also build anything, I asked him to bring his tools. When I was growing up, he remodeled our family room, built a garage, and fixed every broken piece of furniture.

We had a lovely anniversary weekend in Harper's Ferry, West Virginia. Our children loved the days with their grandparents. My dad fixed the shelves and the picnic table. He did not add extra shelves in unwanted places. My mom did not reorganize closets or cabinets to suit her taste. Neither of them negated rules that worked for our family. Mutual respect and love created a trusted space between us.

In a similar manner, we care for one another in the church. When we have a need, we let the extended family know. We talk. We figure out details and then respond appropriately.

It would be a bad idea, for example, to arrive at my sister's home because someone told me her house needed painting. The situation would further deteriorate if I showed up with old, leftover paint. "No worries, we'll just shake it up!" And she shouldn't be concerned about the color. After all, my labor and supplies are free.

Would anyone actually do this to a family member?

Yet this is how some short-term mission teams treat our extended Christian family. They barge in like a kooky aunt or a demanding father prescribing cures to the mission field staff. They veto plans, laugh at paint color choices, and take shortcuts to finish construction for the Friday photo op.

We can do so much better. When a short-term team has a close relationship with the missionary, they don't insult the neighbors, turn their noses up at the food, or rearrange the furniture. Team members bring gifts for ministry as well as special treats like peanut butter or the latest books for the family. As visitors in their home, the team listens humbly and comes prepared to meet the needs as determined by the missionary.

When in relationship, missionaries, in turn, serve as gracious hosts preparing for the arrival of extended family. Although hosting the short-term mission team means additional work, they receive the team with joy. Their visit is the fruition of their invitation extended during last year's furlough stopover at the church. Without hesitation, they trust the team to provide high-quality programming for the children they are discipling. Their musical abilities and teaching gifts will enhance the after-school ministry as well as give the missionary a needed break. One of the days, though, they want to take a day off and bring the team to the mountain peak overlooking their village. They want to share the beauty of God's creation with their visiting family.

Our call to "go and make disciples" requires the work of the entire church. Not just your church or my church. God expects the entire body of Christ to function as one to take the gospel message to all peoples. The multifaceted Great Commission depends on the diverse gifts and talents represented throughout the global church: "For just as each of us has one body with many members, and these members do not all have the same function, so in Christ we, though many, form one body, and each member belongs to all the others. We have different gifts, according to the grace given to each of us" (Romans 12:4-6).

Short-term mission teams can avoid harm through humble listening and selfless action. "For by the grace given me I say to every one of you: Do not think of yourself more highly than you ought, but rather think of yourself with sober judgment" (Romans 12:3). Teams sacrificially give time and resources; missionaries open their lives and ministries. Selflessly we serve one another.

Nearly every short-term mission training curriculum includes the Great Commission (Matthew 28:18-20) in its lesson plan. Yes, the team is indeed part of God's sending. Our presence on the mission field, however, is as a nanosecond to the career missionaries' decades. A change in mindset is needed.

The foundational Scripture passage for the first mission team I led was Micah 6:8. Our work and devotionals focused on the Old Testament prophet's description of what God requires of us: to act justly, love mercy, and walk humbly. Brian Howell proposed this verse as the basis for every church's theology of short-term mission. I couldn't agree more! Howell explained that "our guiding narrative should be one of humility and fellowship even more than service and sacrifice."

Reflection from a Paraguayan pastor brings the theory into practice. "On the basis of relationship, we, as Latin American Christians, would like short-term mission groups to keep coming. Not to teach us how to evangelize, or how to work correctly or efficiently in the church, but to live with us, get to know us, have fellowship together and thus, living together, to learn from one another and teach each other."

The best short-term mission leaders work closely with mission partners in the field to balance opportunity for spiritual growth with the ministry tasks. Short-term missions do indeed create a unique environment for transformation. Team members combine their gifts and talents to serve as one body. Shared experiences of sleeping on air mattresses separated by mere inches and cooking together for twenty quickly create lasting bonds.

In this petri dish of instant community, God does extraordinary work. The new daily routines and expectant hearts stir souls into a teachable posture. Trust forms among team members. Personal facades melt away. In morning devotions and evening debriefs, an effective short-term mission leader draws attention relentlessly back to the Lord and his work. We begin to see one another in spirit and in truth. Our increased appreciation of each person on the team and in the mission's community enables us to embrace God's command to love one another. It is a significant step on the path toward spiritual maturity.

Improving post-project efforts would also extend the benefit of short-term mission teams. As difficult as they are to schedule, follow-up meetings with team members allow critical processing of experiences. The discussions help integrate faith lessons into lives back home. Because periods of frustration often follow the spiritual mountain-top experiences of short-term missions, walking together helps everyone pass through the valley. In the field, missionaries need to follow up with those served by the team. Opportunities for conversation abound after a team leaves! New friendships testify to God's global family but can also lead to a sense of abandonment. The local churches who send and those who host both bear the responsibility of short-term mission aftercare.

As we commit to the paradigm of community along with doing due diligence in preparation, short-term mission projects can be an effective tool for missional engagement. Intentional choice in this continuum moves ministry forward and reduces potential harm. A helpful tool for understanding effective short-term missions is the Standards of Excellence (SOE) in Short-Term Missions. Nearly twenty years ago, leaders from churches and mission agencies agreed on seven best practices for churches and short-term mission agencies. This list includes God-centeredness, empowering partnerships, mutual design, comprehensive administration, qualified leadership, appropriate training, thorough follow-through.

Every church needs to determine their place on the short-term mission continuum. Is your church supportive of sending teams? If so, will you work directly with your mission partners or with third-party short-term mission agencies? Will the primary purpose of short-term mission projects be to disciple team members or to meet specific needs of mission partners? Will church resources—funding, staff time, material contributions—be expended toward organizing teams? The conversation about short-term mission teams will clarify the church's goals and their types of support for mission partners.

How can seven days influence the billions of people who still do not know Jesus? One person at a time. Sometimes a short-term mission team is God's response to the cries of the lost and lonely. One summer several years ago, our church sent out four teams to serve mission partners in different parts of the world. We worked closely with the larger, extended family of Christ to meet many needs.

- To the lonely refugee boy from Nepal, the Lord sent our North Carolina sports ministry team. Soccer and friendship opened the door for him to hear the full story of Jesus.

- To the elderly women and men who could no longer read their Bibles, he sent our Guatemala team to host an eye clinic. They distributed reading glasses that members of our home church had donated.

- To the new church plant reaching an impoverished village, he sent our Yucatan team to purchase supplies and finish the roof over their new building.

- To nearly 150 children orphaned by HIV/AIDS, he sent our team to the African bush. We sat in the dirt with the "least of these." We heard their stories and wrapped our arms around these little ones to be the physical demonstration of the love of Christ.

We rejoiced with new followers of Jesus and with those still exploring their faith. We rested in knowing our partners would follow up. After a thorough assessment of short-term mission projects, Howell determined that "while it is true that short-term mission can be done poorly, with proper training the benefits for both hosts and travelers outweigh the costs." May we learn to serve with intentionality in humility and community.

QUESTIONS

1. Which one of the following scenarios best describes your place on the short-term mission continuum? Choose the one that most closely represents the direction of your calling. From your perspective, what makes your choice the best option?

   ❑ Adam looks for opportunities to participate in short-term mission projects. He assists his church to discover trusted agencies who host teams in locations throughout the world. Developing friendships and experiencing new cultures deepens his understanding of God's kingdom and the church's work worldwide.

   ❑ Beatriz supports short-term teams to respond to specific needs of her church's mission partners. Special requests to bring children's ministry programming and a medical clinic to their South American partner are her next projects to organize.

   ❑ Chris supports mission teams but only those with a dual purpose: to fulfill needs on the mission field and to meet discipling goals for mission team participants. Experienced team leaders—both on the field and from the sending church—are critical to the success of the projects.

   ❑ Dani recognizes value in short-term teams but believes they need to be infrequent. She ensures that her church's mission teams are financially self-supporting and will place minimal demands on missionaries.

   ❑ Eli is not supportive of short-term mission teams, especially not in international locations. He believes the church should expend no resources (funding, staff time, in-kind contributions) toward organizing teams.

2. Rank the scenarios according to your understanding of your church's approach to short-term mission teams. Does the missional engagement compass point toward or away from sending teams?

3. How does the short-term mission direction of your church align with the needs of your mission partners? How has your missions ministry engaged partners in conversation about your church members' abilities and their potential for use in the field?

4. What changes, if any, would you recommend for your church's short-term mission teams? What criteria would you use to assess their value?

6

SERVING THE UNDISCIPLED AND DISCIPLING THE SERVANT

My grocery store never disappoints for social interactions. Last week my cart and I crossed paths with a friend I had not seen in months. After a few minutes of catching up on families, she asked about my church's work with homeless men and women in our community. The conversation went something like this:

"Do you all still do meals at the Lamb Center?" She had helped at the day shelter a couple times the previous year.

"Yes, we serve two meals each month. Would you like to come?" I suggested with a smile. "This Tuesday is our day to make pot roasts."

"Actually, I was asking for my son."

I nodded. "Sure, our group regularly includes teens. We welcome all ages!"

"That's so important." She then launched into the podium speech I had heard countless times from other parents and church leaders alike. "It's good for young people to see firsthand the struggles people face. The teenagers need to understand how truly blessed they are. They take so much for granted. It helps them appreciate all they have at home."

Sigh.

Yes, it's true that many of us take our gifts and blessings for granted. My purpose in partnering with the Lamb Center, however, is not to compel a spirit of gratitude. We serve to help create a welcoming environment where impoverished people can begin taking steps into a sustainable life. The staff, paid and volunteer, build relationships and offer Christ-centered encouragement to every at-risk guest who enters the doors. A beautiful side effect of helping at the shelter is indeed the opportunity for servers to mature. But it is not the primary purpose.

People serve side-by-side with varying motives every day. In most cases, the differences rarely affect a church's missional engagement. When the strategic planning begins, however, the contrasting motives become a source of friction. The means of service may be the same, but the ultimate destinations are radically different.

This chapter's continuum puts words to an undercurrent that derails missional engagement in many congregations: What is the role of the local church in fulfilling the Great Commission? Without a doubt, every Christian is an ambassador for the kingdom. We have already established our shared calling to go and make disciples. This chapter addresses how the church functions in this mandate. Is missional engagement a means to grow the disciples who are sent or to add the souls of those they serve to the kingdom?

The sixth conversation to discovering your church's compass bearing for missional engagement centers on who primarily benefits from the church's missions. Should the church prioritize those who are sent to minister or those who receive that ministry? A missions ministry focused on discipling members through serving differs from a missions ministry focused on reaching the vulnerable. The subtle yet significant difference influences the annual budget (from funding short-term teams to support for new mission partners), church policies, and ministry event planning.

At one end of the continuum is the church whose primary objective is to meet the physical, emotional, and spiritual needs of others. This church sends men and women to rescue children from sex trafficking, serve in disaster recovery zones, and share the gospel in countries hostile to Christianity. Their commitment to the lost exceeds concerns about injury and mortality. A church on this end of the continuum also commits large amounts of resources to evangelistic events and to small groups where people will receive the gospel message. The salvation of these recipients is the *terminus ad quem*, the ultimate purpose, of the church's mission.

At the other end of the continuum is the church whose missional engagement focuses on equipping believers in the local congregation to be the carriers of the gospel message. The leadership pours time and effort into discipling church members. They nurture roots to take hold in the soil of faith, equipping more workers to join in God's work. A healthy congregation—with members mentoring and being mentored—serves kingdom needs selflessly and with perseverance. Their Sunday morning worship is a celebration and family gathering. Visitors experience the power of the gospel through song, word, and love from God's family of faith. Members follow up with conversation and encouragement. The church's passion for nonbelievers emerges in the leadership's investment in members, servants on the front lines with neighbors, coworkers, and others in the community.

Where does your missional engagement compass point: toward the one who brings or the one who receives the gospel message? To examine your church's compass bearing, we will consider the goals at both ends of the continuum. The varied expressions of the calling to go and tell the good news have led to countless misunderstandings. I have found this continuum to be one of the least discussed among church leaders. Perhaps the disconnect lies in the overlap between missions ministry and discipleship (or Christian education) ministry. Many souls await those who would bring the good news. But who can go unless they are discipled and sent?

Admittedly this conversation goes beyond the scope of a missions committee. Overarching churchwide vision and strategic goals are usually prayerfully discerned by the pastoral leadership rather than the missions leadership. The interpretation and implementation of the vision, however, occur at the ministry and staff levels. Until all church leaders come together and work to understand the implications of this continuum, unresolved expectations will continue to exist. The resulting tension creates confusion and ultimately hinders the church's work. This chapter's purpose is to help inform a missions strategy that will align with the church's overall vision, resulting in a beautiful synergy for growth in members and kingdom reach.

As we step into this conversation, the greatest challenge will be an unbiased review of the continuum. Before claiming that your church attends to both sides equally, consider each option and how it shows up in church programming. Most churches lean toward one side of the continuum or the other. Assess whether actual practices align with your stated compass bearing for missional engagement. Every local church leadership cadre needs to answer the question: What is our church's role in fulfilling the Great Commission?

MISSION FOR THE RECIPIENT

Recently I was pushing a cart piled high with books donated by our congregation through the halls of an elementary school located just two miles from our church. Over half the school's students receive free or reduced-price meals, so our church had taken an interest in helping out. As I rounded a corner in the hall, centrifugal force threatened to topple my load. The stack slipped under my fingers. A staff member came around the corner just in time to catch the runaway books escaping my grasp.

"Are you with the church that brings food on Fridays for the children?" She paused to help rearrange the books.

"Yes, I am. Do you need something?"

"No, but thank you. Why do you help this school? Do you have children here?"

"No, my children are in college." Then I continued with the words I have spoken many times before, "Faith in Christ encourages me and our church to be involved in the community." The first time I spoke these words they sounded odd and awkward. How would they be received? Would I offend the very person I hoped to serve? Was I being too sensitive? And yet I meant every word.

"Thank you so much!" She handed me another book. "The parents and children are grateful and it's making a difference in their lives."

The world did not change course that day. For that moment, though, the name of Jesus was heard in the halls of a public school. We embody Christ during this earthly journey. As image-bearers "whatever [we] do, whether in word or deed, [we] do it all in the name of the Lord Jesus, giving thanks to God the Father through him" (Colossians 3:17).

When religious leaders questioned Jesus about the recipients of his message—particularly those on the margins of society—he told the story of a lowly shepherd seeking his lost sheep (Luke 15:4-7). Then he told the story of an impoverished woman rejoicing in the recovery of a lost coin. Finally he told one about an impoverished, prodigal son. No matter the perceived value—sheep, coin, or wayward child—each represents the treasured focus of Jesus' ministry.

Our search and rescue techniques vary. Some of us literally go to the ends of the earth seeking the physically and spiritually vulnerable peoples. Others fervently search within their own community for those who are lost or lacking hope in uncertain circumstances. The kindness of a meal, the patience of a friend, and the voice of truth burst through the darkness to reflect God's light. Missional engagement on this end of the continuum cultivates the space for people to experience God.

Some of the poorest of the world's poor inhabit the streets of Calcutta, India. It is there that a young woman from Albania—now known as Mother Teresa—sensed God's calling to serve. With an all-consuming focus on the needs of others, she extended mercy and dignity to the destitute men and women, valuing their lives above her own comfort and safety. I had the privilege of visiting with the nuns of her Missionaries of Charity in Calcutta. Observing their dedication influenced my understanding of recipient-based ministry. Through the Lord's calling, the nuns have chosen a simple, communal life dedicated to serving others. Their selfless outpouring of love shines the light of Christ in an otherwise very dark place. The recipients of their ministry experience grace-filled compassion with every meal and gentle word.

In addition to providing physical care, we yearn to invite people into the eternal family of God. Whether embodied in compassionate acts of serving meals and providing clothing or spoken in bold sermons and written words, the message of Christ's salvific work remains the priority for the church. We are "to contend for the faith that was once for all entrusted to God's holy people" (Jude 3). In all circumstances, we live as Christ's ambassadors, willing to testify of his goodness and mercy. We will continue to go and tell until there are none left to receive the good news.

Seeker-sensitive churches fall on this end of the continuum. They are heavily invested in creating a setting that welcomes nonbelievers. Contemporary music, shorter sermons, and cutting-edge children's programming work together to form an inspirational and enjoyable worship experience. Removing distractions motivates budget and building decisions—from high-end audio-visual systems to comfortable seating. The pinnacle moment of every gathering is the gospel presentation. They direct all labor, talents, and ministries toward evangelism and the people receiving the good news.

Some would suggest, however, that too much attention on this end of the continuum is detrimental to the global church. One concern is the potential for the bigger-and-better mentality. Figuring out how to top last year's Easter service or the tonnage of the food drive, for example, consumes valuable time and financial resources. Another concern is the lack of attention to rigorous Bible study and spiritual disciplines. When members remain young in their faith, missional engagement and leadership development falters. At what point does care for the servant enter the conversation?

DEVELOPMENT OF THE SERVANT

The church on this end of the continuum prioritizes spiritual growth of members and develops missional engagement as a tool for discipleship. Evidence of God's work, new relationships, and expanded comfort zones provide fertile soil for spiritual growth. The church plans mission events primarily for congregants to explore their gifts and talents. As members assess their abilities and interests, they affirm their uniqueness and God-given potential to serve. Empowered and equipped, members move toward maturity in Christ.

Carolyn Walton, a young marketing professional, went to her first small group with hesitation and without a Bible. Church was usually just a Christmas and Easter event for her, but a friend had invited her to this group. But she went back the next week and then the following week. She bought a Bible. The conversation and study filled a gap in her soul that had long been empty. At one meeting she learned the church's homeless shelter outreach needed volunteers. Carolyn committed to helping on Thursday evenings.

As she served, Carolyn experienced God in new ways. As she put it, "It was like God opened my heart and made me more aware of him and the needs around me." Her hours at the shelter provided the opportunity to live out her faith. Each evening she found herself relying more and more on the Lord's promptings in her interactions with the people in the shelter. Her heart for the lost grew and she soon found herself sharing her experiences and testimony at work. As Carolyn's faith became more evident, her pastor invited her to join the leadership development cohort. Her missional engagement not only provided valuable service at the shelter, but it was a significant catalyst for her spiritual growth.

The discipline of service is among the practices of spiritual life that move us toward maturity. In our willingness to be under the authority of others, be uncomfortable, and endure hardships, our souls are transformed. We learn to walk humbly with our God. In *Celebration of Discipline*, Richard Foster notes that "of all the classical Spiritual Disciplines, service is the most conducive to the growth of humility. . . . In [it] we must experience the many little deaths of going beyond ourselves." Our call to servanthood is undeniable. Jesus told his disciples, "Whoever wants to become great among you must be your servant, and whoever wants to be first must be a slave of all. For even the Son of Man did not come to be served, but to serve, and to give his life as a ransom for many" (Mark 10:43-45). When the church develops opportunities to practice the discipline of service, it enables congregants on their path toward spiritual maturity.

Intentional discipleship is a core value of the church on this end of the continuum. In this familial space, faith incubates. We discover the willingness to die to self, leading us to even greater capacities to serve. Therefore, "let us consider how we may spur one another on toward love and good deeds" (Hebrews 10:24). Community guards tenaciously against pride and causes us to confront envy and jealousy. The fellowship of brothers and sisters teaches valuable lessons about relationships, including the principles of conflict resolution (Matthew 18:15-17). Within the context of a discipling community, we learn to live out the call to servanthood.

The church provides the encouragement and accountability to keep us moving forward. Several years ago I grew frustrated with the lack of progress in our church's relationship with the local schools. The support and enthusiasm of our congregation, however, carried me forward. They met every request for emergency food, clothing donations, and summer reading buddies. Today we are involved in several schools assisting children of all ages, mentoring and connecting regularly with teachers. When surrounded by a faithful family of believers, missional engagement is sustainable.

Working closely with mission partners, we can identify and organize well-conceived opportunities for congregants to explore their gifts and talents. Cooking for shut-ins, knitting baby hats, or singing at a nursing home can be first steps that may become avenues for future ministry. Vacation Bible school may reveal someone's gift of teaching. Baking casseroles for the needy may uncover the gift of mercy. "The more I serve," one church member told me, "the more I learn about myself and about God. I feel that I get more out of serving than what I am giving." The Lord works through the missions of the church to multiply and mature kingdom laborers.

Interestingly, social scientists recognize the benefits of serving. Self-help books often include at least one chapter about helping others. Want to improve your self-esteem? Find a place to volunteer, they say. As you "pay it forward" and "do random acts of kindness," confidence and gratitude grow. High school teachers and court judges alike prescribe community service hours as ways to learn and to give back to the neighborhood.

As Christ-followers we too recognize the role servanthood plays on the road to maturity. We, however, serve to become more like Jesus. Regardless of where we give our time and talent, our goal remains to be God's faithful presence. We do not serve to feel good about ourselves nor to be more appreciative of our own "blessings." These are indeed side benefits, but our goals remain to glorify God, obey his commands, and meet the needs of others.

Developing opportunities to serve lies well within the scope of the local church's missional responsibilities. Churches on this end of the continuum recognize the importance of involving congregants and challenging them to the next level of sacrificial mission. As we serve, we grow. Missional engagement increases as the church disciples members and supports them in their callings. The church, when fulfilling its role to disciple believers, will then thrive and multiply.

FINDING OUR PLACE

At the heart of this chapter's conversation is the role of the local church in missional engagement. How does the local church fulfill its responsibility to evangelize *and* to disciple? Is its focus on those who do not yet know Jesus or on those who tell the good news to those who do not yet know Jesus? Your church's compass bearing to serve may point toward one of the ends or it may point somewhere in the middle. Discussing your compass bearing on this continuum will bring to the fore this often hidden and misunderstood issue before it derails the strategic planning process.

The church is God's instrument to complete his gospel mission. Regardless of theological bent—covenantal, evangelical, Lutheran, Pentecostal, Reformed, or other Christian affiliation—we all recognize the joy-filled yet challenging journey toward spiritual maturity. We take seriously the mandate to bring people onto this path. But how the church uses her resources along the path varies.

The twenty-first-century church is participating in the Great Commission through the most creative means ever experienced in history. Globalization and business ventures have opened doors never before available to the church. The divergence in priorities and practicality of the discipleship and evangelism roles can be beneficial in the spread of the gospel message. Healthy Christian communities can be found throughout this servant-recipient continuum. Some churches do both well. Others emphasize one end of the continuum but are wisely attentive to the potential drawbacks and adjust accordingly.

The missions work of the church that prioritizes evangelism looks different than the work of the church that most highly values discipling believers. In programming, for example, the recipient-focused church spends large sums of money on Halloween's alternative Trunk-or-Treat event to reach unbelievers while the servant-focused church spends heavily on the fall leadership summit to equip members to be the frontline of outreach. In both churches the missional engagement goal is to bring new people into God's kingdom.

The key to success is awareness of pitfalls and the ability to respond to them. The church focused on the recipient, for example, can be more intentional about encouraging personal evangelism alongside event-based and small group–based evangelism. When the local church fulfills the role of evangelist, members may relinquish their responsibility in the conversation. The church absolves members of their personal role by being the teller of the good news. Resources and efforts focus on the large-group, seeker-sensitive gatherings so the professional clergy can share the gospel.

The church can better equip members to evangelize. We tend to shy away from talking about religion and politics. A LifeWay Research study recently found "80 percent of those who attend church one or more times a month believe they have a personal responsibility to share their faith. Yet despite this conviction, 61 percent have not told another person about how to become a Christian in the previous six months." The church can help in these discussions by equipping members to tell their faith stories, to explore ways to turn a conversation toward spiritual topics, and to understand the beliefs of other religions and worldviews.

The recipient-focused church will expand their influence by enabling and empowering members along with hosting seeker-friendly events. Scripture calls us to nurture and disciple those in our care.

"Well, hello!" I greeted old friends as we nearly passed one another in the mall.

"Hi! I've been meaning to call you." Laura exchanged a bittersweet look with her husband. "We're looking for a new church and wanted to talk to you about your church."

Dan continued, "The seeker focus of our church is not so good for us anymore. We're looking for ways to go deeper in our faith."

"Have you talked with your pastor?" I asked.

"Yes. He reminded us that our church is focused unapologetically on reaching the unchurched." Laura explained.

"That's a well-defined missions strategy." I nodded.

"Yes, but I would like to learn more about the Bible and ways to share my faith." Dan explained, "The church expects members to grow through serving on Sunday mornings or leading mid-week groups. And there's very little leadership training."

Laura added, "When we invite friends to worship or big events, they are impressed with the music and the preaching. The church works hard to create an atmosphere where people can hear the gospel. But we have no Bible studies and we don't do any missions beyond our own neighborhoods."

When the church does not invest in members, kingdom labor is lost. The Lord has plans for each member of the body. As we exercise our talents, we mature in our faith and bear fruit.

Challenges exist at the other end of the continuum as well. When the church views missional engagement only as the means to disciple members, ministries can become too inward focused. The high value placed on education results in dedicated scholars of the Word. The unintended result, however, can be members who continually feel unqualified to participate in kingdom work. They want one more Bible study before they feel ready to lead a small group or to serve on a mission team. Increased knowledge without action is like a weightlifter who works out at the gym for hours every day. He becomes so preoccupied with his reps and his weight machines that he lacks the vision to see how to use his strength to help others.

Another challenge for the servant-focused church is the potential for ineffective and even harmful results of their ministry. The primary purpose of their missions activities is to maximize the number of opportunities to serve. Despite the win for the church in increasing member involvement, the disconnect with the community's needs may adversely affect the people they serve. An annual day of serving does not a missional church make. Understanding the needs of the recipients is primary for effective missional engagement. The church will have greater kingdom influence when it pays more attention to a ministry's effectiveness in the receiving community.

When missions become a mere tool for spiritual growth, the missions ministry is reduced to the organizer of service-oriented field trips. Metrics of successful missional engagement include the number of members who serve, total backpacks collected, and donations received for the missions fund. The church views every service activity as an opportunity to grow, therefore new slots equal a win. Mission partnerships become less critical. Stories of the family that is no longer homeless, or the formerly incarcerated man who has found employment, or those who have come to faith in Christ are not necessarily highlighted as fulfilling this kind of strategic plan. But a shift to measuring quality changes rather than activity would put the celebration and focus on the recipients and what God is doing in their lives.

The servant-focused church can also unwittingly create an environment where motives other than furthering God's global mission thrive. Desire to proclaim the kingdom can become secondary to a wide range of other participant expectations. Over the years, I have stumbled into people's alternative motives and their attempts to draw me—or the ministries I lead—into their intentions. Some seek personal development such as gaining a skill, adding to a resume, or the warm glow of volunteering. Others may pursue power or influence such as gaining a voice in spending, access to ministry leadership, expanded social network, or their name (or their loved one's name) on the donor recognition wall. Others may just want a tax deduction. While alternative motives are not necessarily harmful or unethical, it is unfair to add these expectations to a missionary's job description.

Effective missional engagement is not self-serving. For the glory of God alone, we balance seeking the lost and equipping the workers. Faith and maturity remain the Christ-centered goals for every congregation, not just the fulfillment of personal potential and increased membership of the local church. Spiritual maturity sustains missional engagement. Hence the long process before sending a missionary into the field. Enthusiasm and availability are not substitutes for maturity and preparation. The tolls on family and community have been high when missions outpace maturity.

As we discern our place on the servant-recipient continuum, we may discover the need to change the focus of some church activities. The annual church picnic, for example, can be refocused to the recipient end as members are encouraged to invite friends who do not yet know Jesus. The small groups in a seeker-friendly church could launch a series on spiritual disciplines. The servant-focused curriculum could introduce ancient contemplative practices to encourage growth and a deeper understanding of God. New life can be breathed into ongoing rhythms of the church as you align your compass bearing to serve.

Each faith community has a specific role in God's kingdom purposes. When we discern our role and articulate goals, we can proceed forward with less conflict. Even as we locate ourselves on the continuum, we recognize the responsibility to be attentive to the needs of both recipients and servants. Spiritual growth most effectively emerges in congregations where everyone is both being fed and feeding others.

QUESTIONS

1. Which one of the following scenarios best describes your place on the servant-recipient continuum? Choose the one that most closely represents the direction of your calling. From your perspective, what makes your choice the best option?

❏ Andre views missions as a tool for discipleship of believers. He and his church plan missional engagement primarily for congregants to explore their gifts and talents. They empower members to then go and be Christ's ambassadors where the Lord calls them.

❏ Brigitte desires to work with mission agencies who include spiritual growth of participants as one of their goals, although not the primary goal. Training and debriefing are important aspects of her ministry model.

❏ Craig views the role of the church as equally invested in discipling members and in evangelizing the lost. He most desires to partner with mission agencies and missionaries who balance their ministry toward both the not-yet-believers on the mission field and the volunteers from their church.

❏ Donnella prefers to work with mission agencies who include evangelism as a primary goal. Her motivation for missions is to share the gospel message but also to equip others to give their testimonies and to tell the good news.

❏ Eric views evangelism as the church's primary role in missions. Time and resources should focus on welcoming not-yet-believers into the family of God. Church members can pursue Bible study, webinars, and discipleship conferences outside the scope of church activities. These resources are readily available throughout the country.

2. Rank the scenarios according to your faith community's understanding of the church's role in missional engagement. Give examples to support your ranking.

3. Do the expectations of the church leadership and the missions ministry align? If not, how would you describes the differences? How might a conversation begin to consider alternative options?

4. How does your church's role in discipleship and evangelism align with the philosophy of ministry of your mission partners?

7

MINIMIZING AND
EMBRACING RISK

I n July 2007 our missions meeting concluded in prayer for a South
Korean short-term team being held hostage by Muslim extremists. The
team of twenty had arrived in Afghanistan planning to volunteer in a
school and to provide medical aid. Three missionaries already in the
country joined them for their projects. The Taliban kidnapped the team
shortly after their arrival and would eventually kill two of the hostages
before South Korea agreed to the political and financial demands for
their release.

Around the world mixed emotions surrounded the kidnapping of the
team. Outrage at the violence brought many people to their knees in prayer.
Others, however, questioned the team's presence in the war-torn country.
Disapproval of the team and their sending church filled news articles, conference seminars, and church hallways.

The churches of South Korea are highly committed to mission work.
Sacrificially serving around the world, they remain among the top-ten
sending countries in the world. No one questioned the South Korean
team's motives or their heart for God, but their lack of situational awareness
and crisis preparedness led many to reexamine crosscultural service.

The team's abduction complicated ministry for years, not only for the South Korean missions community but for others worldwide as well.

When is the risk too high? My colleagues who opposed the team's presence in Afghanistan pointed out their naiveté, along with their lack of regard to the political climate and security concerns. Others supported their call to serve, reminding me that our calling as Christian witnesses includes being faithful even unto death (Revelation 2:10). The team's capture and the killing of two team members also drew attention to the brutality of the Taliban against the Afghan people. By its very nature, missional engagement is not safe. God calls us to the dark places to shine his light and make his name known. Danger lurks in human depravity as well as in the unseen realm of spiritual battles.

Often the first question I am asked when considering a new missional engagement is some version of "Is it safe?" The answer is never the comforting, "Yes, we will be perfectly fine." In addition to not knowing the future, risk will always be part of the church's mission. Crosscultural interactions place us in situations that can become perilous for any number of reasons. Negative reactions to the gospel range from rude indifference to hostile persecution. The question should instead be: How much risk am I willing to bear? Somewhere between the cautious counting of costs and the reckless stepping out in faith, ministry inches forward. This chapter examines our approach to risk and its repercussions in our Great Commission calling.

What is the role of risk in a church's missional engagement? Is counting the cost better than a leap-of-faith strategy? What is the price of hesitation? Of impulsiveness? Is it possible that "safety" has become an obstacle to the Great Commission? Is it also possible that extreme risk takers have caused damage in the name of Jesus by ignoring wise counsel?

The final conversation for discovering your compass bearing for missional engagement focuses on risk. The continuum stretches from the safety of minimizing risk to the dauntless support of ministry in hazardous settings. Does the potential for harm halt missional engagement? When measured by the world's standards, risk weighs the probability of an accident with the consequences in loss of health or money or other physical and emotional injury. The likelihood of negative outcomes causes hesitation. Do the complexity and the mental exhaustion of poverty, for example, reduce our response to homelessness initiatives? Those willing to risk the emotional costs discover the value of the investment despite the pain of uncovered prejudices and the hard labor of community transformation.

On one end of the continuum, missional engagement minimizes risk. It's a place where ministry can thrive in confidence and low anxiety. The environment provides reliability and stability that benefit both the believer and the nonbeliever. As Christ-followers, we come by this yearning for shalom quite naturally. The kingdom of God offers peace and reconciliation to all who call on the name of Jesus. We represent this kingdom with our very being and desire its reality to the ends of the earth. Our placement at this end of the continuum clarifies settings where we best flourish in our call to serve others.

On the other end of the continuum is high-risk missional engagement. Dauntless believers recognize the difficulties of the calling but choose to go nonetheless. It's the place where hard discussions begin and hostile actions may erupt. Harm may come in our local communities as well as in crosscultural locations. We recognize nothing is safe about this world. Our position at this end of the continuum reveals a greater tolerance for risk. We are willing to risk everything, even life itself, for the sake of the gospel.

While the previous continuums focused on the mission work itself, this continuum encourages a look inward. Our views of risk influence decisions every day. The potential for harm and the efforts to avoid harm can draw both visceral reactions and calculated responses. If your church begins a calling to serve the persecuted church, for example, your place on the "safe" end of the continuum may need revising. Prayer and discernment will help identify concerns and needs in order to resolve the conflict in goals. Are we willing to pause in the discomfort long enough to examine the tension?

Does your missional engagement compass point toward a place of low or high risk? To determine your compass bearing, we will assess personal risk alongside the gospel mandate. We will also consider the role fear plays in our decisions and how it can counter the promises of Scripture. God sends us into many different places, requiring different levels of comfort. Courage, meanwhile, takes many forms, including perseverance in the mundane and trials in hazardous places. As we pursue this final conversation, consider not only your present location on the continuum but also the possibility of increased risk tolerance through risk management's best practices.

AVOIDING RISK

Through the church, missional engagement cultivates the kingdom landscape in our neighborhoods and beyond. We work to create this space for people to experience God's presence and healing. God establishes communities of believers to represent his kingdom on earth. He intends our mutual care for one another to meet needs. Churches around the world daily provide housing, make meals, and offer financial assistance for families in crisis. We thrive and mature in the peace and stability of healthy churches.

Within the church, we expect our leaders to minimize risk. Through rigorous reviews and carefully crafted policies, we strive to have a safe church. We establish safety protocols for working with children, maintain fire alarms in our buildings, and keep church vans in good working order. Church leaders regularly assess potential for hazards. Careful planning and ongoing attentiveness ensure the greatest levels of safety and security for our church family and friends. We want to maintain a safe place for worship and fellowship.

When Jesus sent his disciples to preach the good news, he told them to "be as shrewd as snakes and as innocent as doves" (Matthew 10:16). They would need to be attentive to the hazards around them. Although danger awaited, he counseled them to not pursue unnecessary risk. "If anyone will not welcome you or listen to your words, leave that home or town and shake the dust off your feet" (Matthew 10:14). Jesus expected them to be wise and ever watchful in fulfilling their ministry.

Undoubtedly, some degree of risk comes whenever we engage the needs around us. Our responses will vary not only with our abilities, but also our capacities for the different types of risk we may encounter. Physical hazards may involve perilous roads in developing countries, rehab of dilapidated homes, or violence on urban streets. Emotional risks can be related to anxiety of the unknown, guilt about personal actions, or stress of intense community life. Spiritual risks of doubt, persecution, or demonic influences further threaten the safety of those who serve. Risk analysis seeks to mitigate the hazards in order to more effectively serve God's kingdom.

Surrounded by abject poverty, emotional risk overtook unprepared members of a short-term mission team serving in Africa. I visited the orphan ministry where they had served. In their wake they left tearful children and a distressed staff. At least two of the team members had promised to adopt children, even telling them to change their last names. Adoption, however, was not possible in this situation. The local missionaries faced long hours seeking to restore peace in the children's lives. Unable to cope, these team members had responded out of their own pain rather than out of appropriate care for the children.

As the church moves forward in missional engagement, adequate planning and risk assessment are critical. The careful review of potential risk benefits both the church and the missionary. With today's technology, a plethora of resources are at our fingertips. Newspapers from all corners of the planet publish articles online. Experts in every field of study upload articles, podcasts, and webinars daily. The US Department of State and Center for Disease Control websites supply health and safety updates regularly. As we serve, we remain attentive to the political climate and cultural changes to avoid negligent behavior. Risk assessments reveal the scope of hazards a church would need to accept to move forward with a ministry.

Churches on this end of the continuum recognize the risks for their congregants. Careless and uninformed decisions can result in tragic consequences. Inadequate safety protocols on home rehab sites, for example, can lead to physical injuries. Power tools and rusty nails have shortened the workday for many helpers. The leadership chooses to keep members out of harm's way by allowing only carefully controlled opportunities to serve.

The church that prioritizes risk avoidance is also aware of the burden of short-term workers on ministry partners. Whether serving breakfast at a shelter or teaching in a week-long vacation Bible school, training is important and will reduce risks. Naive workers can cause more problems than they solve. Instruction before, during, and after the service project creates a valuable learning environment and space for spiritual growth. As a visiting church, we want to bring peace and not add to the challenges through risky behaviors.

A strategy that aligns well with churches on this end of the continuum is indigenous partnerships. New opportunities arise daily to connect with believers serving unreached people in their native lands. In some cases, their ministry may offer the only avenue for kingdom work in their country. Intercessory prayer and financial support provide the resources and encouragement that best benefit both the missionary and the not-yet-believers. Some indigenous missionaries will occasionally host small short-term teams for specialized purposes, such as medical missions.

An ongoing, systematic, and honest evaluation honors God's purposes for kingdom work.

> The prudent see danger and take refuge,
>> but the simple keep going and pay the penalty. (Proverbs 22:3)

Every decision affects time, money, and relationships. Missionaries, congregants, and church leaders are affected. Their careful stewardship monitors and allows continued ministry even in the most tenuous situations. With policies in place for local and international locations, including contingency plans, child protection policy, and crisis training, we mitigate risk to be able to focus on kingdom work.

Amid all these security protocols, however, a new risk enters. In his book *Risk Is Right*, John Piper asks, "Are you caught in the enchantment of security, paralyzed from taking any risk for the cause of God?" Minimized risk may reduce liability for the church, but are we truly preparing our congregation for the sacrificial service intended for the life of a disciple?

DAUNTLESS RISK

I admit I struggle to align the cost of discipleship with my desire to protect friends and family. Nevertheless, total risk avoidance is incompatible with the church's mission.

Scripture extols the bold faith and risk demonstrated by God's people. God gave the call to action and they responded. Abraham moved his family to an unknown, crosscultural destination. Moses' parents risked death by hiding him from authorities. The people of Israel faced drowning as they traversed the temporarily dry Red Sea. Jesus' disciples preached the good news and suffered deadly consequences. In the midst of great trials, Paul proclaimed to the elders in Ephesus, "I consider my life worth nothing to me; my only aim is to finish the race and complete the task the Lord Jesus has given me—the task of testifying to the good news of God's grace" (Acts 20:24). They each stepped out in faith, despite lacking a risk assessment or crisis-management plan.

Risk cuts to the core of our faith in God and our missional engagement. Do we trust God's plan? John Piper describes the Christ-follower's risk as

> not heroism, or the lust for adventure, or the courage of self-reliance, or the need to earn God's good will, but rather faith in the all-providing, all-ruling, all-satisfying Son of God, Jesus Christ. The strength to risk losing face for the sake of Christ is the faith that God's love will lift up your face in the end and vindicate your cause. The strength to risk losing money for the cause of the gospel is the faith that we have treasure in the heavens that cannot fail. The strength to risk losing life in this world is faith in the promise that he who loses his life in this world will save it for the age to come.

Churches on this end of the continuum willingly walk into dangerous ministry. The high tolerance for risk allows for partnerships in hostile and difficult places. They are bold in their efforts and give little heed to warnings of physical harm. With the peace of Christ and assurance of his presence, they partner and go where people are not yet committed to Christ. They proclaim Jesus in Muslim-majority nations, speak out for the rights of the marginalized, and hand out Bibles even at the risk of arrest or death itself.

Sometimes God's call for risk is within our own community. Fairfax Community Church is committed to being a witness for the kingdom in their neighborhood. When their northern Virginia region became a hub for refugee resettlement, they took the risk of getting involved. The congregation committed to helping new arrivals—Christians, Muslims, and those of no particular religion—with language skills, employment, transportation, and general relocation needs. The church's heart for the marginalized overruled the risk of resistance from immigration opponents. The resulting crosscultural relationships are improving the lives of refugees as well as transforming the hearts and minds of congregation members.

Believers move forward through risk by mastering the fear it generates. We begin by seeking the Lord's guidance. The boldness we lack is found in the gift of the Holy Spirit: "For the Spirit God gave us does not make us timid, but gives us power, love and self-discipline" (2 Timothy 1:7). Lists of pros and cons cannot bring the assurance of God's presence nor safety from harm. It is through our faith in Christ, confident in the promises of Scripture, that we can go.

> So we say with confidence,
>> "The Lord is my helper; I will not be afraid.
>> What can mere mortals do to me?" (Hebrews 13:6)

Physical harm may come our way—indeed many have died for the sake of the gospel—but nothing will ever separate us from the priceless, eternal treasure of "the love of God that is in Christ Jesus our Lord" (Romans 8:38-39).

Churches on this end of the continuum do not allow fear to direct their steps. They are aware of the potential hazards, but go nonetheless. Risk is not a barrier to pursuing God's call for these congregations. With eyes wide open and hearts fully committed, the influence of risk is minimized. Their actions may be perceived as reckless or even dangerous by some. Yet their choices are faithful to their understanding of God's sovereignty and control. They are fulfilling their call to high-risk ministry.

Minimized risk in the comfort zone holds only the slightest allure. Unusual food, cold showers, and large insects do not deter missional engagement. Comfort and safety are not the goals. When Peter attempted to keep Jesus safe from harm, Jesus called out the influence of darkness. Fear, instead of the nature of God, had flooded Peter's mind. Jesus then offered his guiding theme for this end of the continuum: "Whoever wants to be my disciple must deny themselves and take up their cross and follow me. For whoever wants to save their life will lose it, but whoever loses their life for me and for the gospel will save it. What good is it for someone to gain the whole world, yet forfeit their soul?" (Mark 8:34-36).

Risk edges us out of our comfortable places. When we step into cultures unlike our own, we become the humble student. The challenges, confrontations, and even the wrong turns present valuable lessons toward spiritual maturity. We do indeed risk hardship and failure, but lingering in stagnant ease precludes answering God's call to serve.

I was struck by a poster I saw hanging in a church lobby that said, "Safe in the palm of God's hand." Meant to encourage dramatic leaps of faith, the message instead misinterprets or even trivializes the hardships some believers endure. Was the student who broke his arm on the mission project not really a Christian? Was the missionary who died of dengue fever outside God's will? Job's story illustrates that harm befalls even those who love the Lord and are serving him faithfully. When safety and security form the foundation of our theology of risk, we have moved beyond the theology of the Bible.

Safety is not promised in this life. Churches on this end of the continuum recognize this reality. Scripture says nothing about protection from physical harm by being in the palm of God's hand or the arms of Jesus. Instead, we find story after story of men and women who suffered terribly and died tragically while squarely in the center of God's will.

In her book *Facing Danger*, Anna Hampton writes, "When called by God to unsafe places, we won't let fear paralyze us because God is always with us (Joshua 1:9; Psalm 91; Isaiah 43)." The kingdom is worth the risk. We live in a dark and dangerous world. Crises come to believers and non-believers alike. We choose to remain obedient to our call to be God's ambassadors in all places at all times, trusting he is present and at work in all circumstances. He is and always will be with us even to the end of the age.

FINDING OUR PLACE

Risk is and always will be part of the Great Commission. Through the ages and around the globe, God's kingdom has advanced through Christ-followers who choose the narrow path for the sake of the gospel.

The twenty-first-century church faces hard discussions about prejudices and hostilities. These are some of the final roadblocks to reaching every nation. Too often, however, fear derails our efforts. Our best course of action is to face fear with prayer, conversation, and research. Only then will it lose influence over our decisions. When we stop avoiding the tensions, we can better identify and overcome the sources of our discomfort. After several unsuccessful attempts to share the gospel with an atheist friend, for example, I realized my fear of rejection was the source of my problem. It made a spiritual conversation feel too risky. Recognizing the source of my discomfort is helping me move beyond it. Risk will always be present, but fear and the resulting tensions decrease.

The risk-averse and litigious nature of our Western mindset propels church leaders toward the safety end of the continuum. They may even dismiss the biblical mandate to go if the going requires a passport. When extreme risk aversion drives missional engagement, serving the materially and spiritually poor becomes drive-by ministry. The time and emotional energy needed for sustainable transformation is seen as a speculative risk better left to the social services experts. Sharing the gospel at work is reduced to leaving a stack of flyers for the Christmas Eve worship services on the front desk because the risk of offending coworkers is too high to turn a conversation to spiritual topics. Funds donated to missions are negligible and considered imprudent; a suitable retirement nest egg supersedes generosity toward kingdom purposes.

New Hope Fellowship, a local congregation of mostly poor and homeless members, is one of my church's mission partners. Their worship and their people are raw and honest. They respond in truth when greeted with the one-syllable salutation, "Hi-how-are-you?" I hear details of the rain-soaked tent, a killer toothache, the latest eviction notice, and other pressing matters. I stumble in my response. Sometimes the deepest divide in our society is the socioeconomic one.

Brian and Marci Swanson, who served as our missions liaisons with New Hope, proposed a radical idea: let's host the congregation at our church on a Sunday. We could invite them to our worship service, serve lunch, and follow up with a movie. Being hypothermia season, it would be a blessing to the roughly eighty members of New Hope to not have to return to the emergency shelters until evening.

Red flags of concern popped up everywhere as we considered the idea. Yes, we wanted to welcome New Hope to our church home. But how do you blend a homeless community with middle- to upper-class suburban families? New Hope members carry belongings in black trash bags and fraying backpacks. Their layered clothes are unwashed and odorous. Unemployed felons and men and women with unresolved mental health diagnoses call New Hope their home. Some are Christian, others are not; but they come because of the love and acceptance in the church community.

After much prayer and discussion of the needs of both congregations, we decided to extend the invitation. It was a leap of faith for both churches. Risk of rejection had driven New Hope members away from previous traditional, suburban churches. Risk of harm causes many in our church family to avoid people on the fringes of society. We began our preparation by educating our congregation about poverty and its consequence. We invited their help to make our New Hope guests feel welcome. We also made some practical adjustments—increased the number of greeters in the lobby, added missions committee members to the hallways of the children's classrooms, and placed ashtrays by doors.

It was worth the risk. In fact, we now host our New Hope friends annually. This year was our sixth gathering. More of our members have become involved with their congregation beyond our annual gathering. We know one another better now. We pray for each other and celebrate milestones: new jobs, new places to live, sobriety anniversaries. This gathering has helped bridge the gap between the wealthy and the more vulnerable people in our community. It continues to be worth the risk.

Indeed, the church has a responsibility to examine risks before partnering with or sending a missionary. Department of State warnings, insurance company policies, and social services advice provide valuable input, but as Hampton recognizes, "The Holy Spirit's leading is the one overarching guide in risk analysis and management." Spirit-led guidance emerges when humble hearts unite in prayer, steeped in Scripture. As we welcome the Lord into the process, we begin to move away from the demands of the culturally created safety zone and into a space of calculated risk.

The apostle Paul demonstrated risk mitigation tactics in his missionary journeys. At various times, he avoided risk, limited his exposure to it, transferred it to others, or accepted it. Hampton cautions against seeking to emulate Paul's tactics. She writes, "Instead, our primary focus here needs to be on how he heard the Holy Spirit. While Paul sets for us an excellent example in Christian vocational risk, his guide and ours always is the Holy Spirit." Through disciplines of worship, prayer, and fasting, Paul and his travel companions called on the Lord for guidance. When we commit to being a community united in prayer for missional engagement, we become more attentive to the Spirit and to his direction for high-risk ministry.

After the commitment to prayer, the next step to understanding our place on this continuum is to work through a risk analysis. Research increases awareness of the potential for harm and enables effective preparation for a possible crisis. A better understanding of both the positive and negative outcomes increases our capacity for risk. Help is available for the process of gathering information for a risk assessment. Mission agencies and denominational offices offer questionnaires, guidelines, and even coaches to walk a church through best practices.

Hampton describes one well-known risk assessment model that centers on three primary questions: (1) What can go wrong? (2) What is the likelihood of that happening? (3) What are the consequences? When using this model, consider all possible scenarios for each question. Factor in crosscultural issues, transportation concerns, personnel aspects, weather risks, and so on. Continued prayerful discussion on acceptable and unacceptable risks for your church needs to follow. Differences in risk tolerance will emerge in the conversation. It will be important to separate personal preference from the church's divine calling. Many of us struggle with risk in our own lives and project this difficulty onto the church's mission work. Careful assessment will demonstrate the difference between calculated risk and foolish risk, helping to move our cautious selves off the sunshine couch and into the mission field.

After completing a risk assessment, we next create a risk management system. Many tools exist to help shape your plan. Insurance companies, mission agencies, and internet searches can provide a plethora of examples. Needed components include a child-protection policy, facility security, an evacuation plan, a shelter-in-place plan, and a crisis-management team. These components help mitigate risk for you and your church family.

Beyond assessments and systems, the community created by a healthy church is the greatest asset to reducing the risk inherent in our call to fulfill the Great Commission. God's plan for global mission rests in the context of the body of Christ. To go and serve without a safety net of relationships is one of the greatest risks of all. The capacity for risk improves immensely when we have community.

Our connections with one another increase security by expanding our networks of options and opportunities. Inspiration to solve problems multiplies in the camaraderie of others. Shared resources—including possessions and knowledge—increase the potential for success. Being present and carrying one another's burdens reduces vulnerability to fear and intimidation. Frederick Buechner explained, "Wherever people love each other and are true to each other and take risks for each other, God is with them and for them and they are doing God's will." Herein lies a critical role for the church. When surrounding fellow believers with support, a healthy community can equip and send many workers into the mission field.

Maybe we need to live on the edge a little bit more. For kingdom purposes, how can we be more risky with God's gifts? In the parable of the talents, the businessman praised his servants who made seemingly reckless investments with his money (Matthew 25:14-30). The servant who made the conservative, risk-averse choice received severe admonishment. His failure to take action ultimately led to his banishment. May we never be so accused!

Jesus invites us into his yoke. We share the load with the Lord of Lords. "Come to me, all you who are weary and burdened, and I will give you rest" (Matthew 11:28). We need not fret but find rest for our souls and our work in him. Our job description as Christ's witnesses does not change in the face of challenges. We submit our fears to him. Yoked and committed to Christ, we trust him to bring his plans to completion even when we are at risk of harm.

Where is your church on the risk continuum? Do you develop disciples who are risk averse or risk takers? Risk is inherent in each step of missional engagement. We will be displaced from our comfort zones. But the call is different for each person and each congregation. How are the gifts of the congregation best suited to serve God's mission in low-, medium-, or high-risk ministry? God's invitation to the narrow road awaits. Margot Starbuck writes,

> There are noticeably fewer travelers on this narrow road. . . . Everyone who has chosen to travel the skinny road is there because they're willing to be less comfortable than they would be on the highway. They know that there will be bumps and bends and breakdowns. Some will lose air-conditioning. Some will have to get out of their vehicles and actually walk. The reason they're even there is because, when they noticed Jesus pulling off the highway, they took the risk of trailing right behind him.

QUESTIONS

1. Which one of the following scenarios best describes your place on the risk continuum? Choose the one that most closely represents your risk tolerance. From your perspective, what makes your choice the best option?

❑ Aisha agrees with her church's goal of minimizing risk for church members in missional engagement. She believes ministry thrives in high confidence and minimal anxiety. The environment provides reliability and stability to benefit both the believer and the not-yet-believer.

❑ With input of risk assessments and wise counsel, Bill is willing to undertake somewhat risky missional engagements. He and his church begin to nudge people out of their comfort zone while also maintaining a cautious, responsible posture.

❑ Catalina desires to count the cost for missional engagements. Risk is one of the factors but not the decisive one when considering a commitment to serve. When called, she is willing to consider moving forward in ministry despite some potential risk.

❑ Through prayer and in the context of community, Dong Hwa is willing to consider partnerships with medium-risk ministries. Longevity of relationships and competence in ministry weigh heavily in his decision making.

❑ Elise and her church have a high tolerance for risk. They partner with ministries in hazardous locations, pursuing a risk-filled calling. She supports members participating in high-risk missional engagements who recognize the difficulties of the calling but choose to go nonetheless.

2. Rank the scenarios with regard to your church's philosophy of risk in missional engagement. Give examples to support your ranking.

3. Do you think reduction of liability is good or bad? Explain. What is the relationship between risk aversion and faith?

4. What assessments would you need in order to consider higher-risk missions initiatives for yourself? For your church?

CONCLUSION

MOBILIZING OUR CONGREGATIONS

Seared into my brain is a moment when I was twenty-five years old and lost in the middle of the woods. I was participating in a nighttime orienteering race across unfamiliar terrain in southern Virginia under a moonless sky. Midpoint in the race, I found myself alone, disoriented, and without a clue which way to go.

Earlier in the evening, the organizers had dropped teams off in staggered locations along the edge of wooded parkland. The destination point was about two miles away. Our team of three huddled over a topographic map to study possible routes. A ten-foot ravine, two creeks, and several small hills lay between us and the pole at the endpoint. We plotted our course. I recorded the compass bearings and translated distances into pace counts.

The whistle blew. We raced into the dark forest, counting steps and glancing at the compass through red-filtered flashlights. Within the first hundred feet, we were on the edge of the ravine. After scooting down then back up the steep gully, we consulted our compass and set out again on the proper directional heading. We continued at our walk-run pace, occasionally slapped by low-hanging branches but feeling smug about our steady progress.

Somehow, though, I became separated from our team. Because it was a race, I kept moving forward, confident we would reconnect. Distracted but still in a race mindset, I stumbled into a massive clump of thorny vines. I tried to push through but further entangled myself in the middle of the hateful plants. They bound my arms, preventing access to my flashlight. Adrenaline fed a rapidly approaching panic attack. I was trapped.

After what felt like an eternity (but was probably closer to five minutes), my teammates' calm voices reached me. They quietly prompted me to drop to my hands and knees and crawl toward their voices. I emerged from my thorny prison disoriented and anxious.

My team got us back onto our charted course. When at last we stepped out of the woods, we were a mere ten feet from the endpoint pole and well within the time limit. Much to our surprise, only two other teams had arrived closer to the pole. A huge victory for us!

When I first stepped into missions ministry, it was like being back in my nighttime orienteering race. With the best of intentions, missions committee members and I set out to make plans. We had funds and people and the desire to serve. Some efforts worked but others did not. I felt disoriented in relation to the church leadership when the means and methods clashed. We stumbled in our attempts to adjust partnerships toward a more focused missions strategy. Without the local-global conversation, for example, we wandered back and forth between initiatives for community outreach and unreached people groups. Without the crisis-sustainability understanding, barbed comments about unhealthy dependence and uncaring hearts created uncomfortable conversations.

We had no structure for evaluating new mission partners. Risk avoidance dominated our decisions about who and where to serve. We lacked the tools to evaluate the uncharted territory of new ministry engagement options. As a result we stepped in many different directions and undertook a wide range of projects. We had the heart to serve but our compass was directionless.

Caught in the thicket, we stopped.

Prayerfully, we began to engage in the seven conversations of missional engagement. One-on-one and in group discussions, we began to develop an intentional path for our congregation. As we wrestled with location and other factors, the discussions also revealed interests and passions. We discovered a heart for vulnerable children and the gift of teaching in many of our members. With a clearer understanding of needs and gifts, we are becoming more effective in navigating our call to kingdom ministry.

Unraveling the complexity of options enables a church to make educated, holistic decisions toward fulfilling the Great Commission and the Great Commandments. No longer are missions events simply items on the calendar. The annual food drive moves from being an isolated event to part of an overall strategy to address local poverty that includes donations of produce from church members' gardens, a job-readiness program, and mentoring. Through these combined initiatives we are reaching vulnerable neighbors with compassion and mercy.

IMPLEMENTING BEST PRACTICES

After laboring through the seven conversations, your church is prepared for its next steps in the strategic planning process. Parameters for missional engagement are guided by where your church lands on each of the continuums. Familiarity with the wide range of possibilities along with the potential tensions creates fertile ground for brainstorming and innovative planning. The process for further refining your direction continues as you learn more about where you are called and with whom you travel. Many resources are available to help guide church leaders through the strategic planning process.

Learn the terrain. First, become well-informed of the needs in the space where the Lord is calling you. In today's connected world, we have access to abundant first-person accounts and well-researched articles. We have much to learn in every crosscultural setting. Uninformed giving and going compounds problems instead of bringing solutions. We are without excuse for ignorance. Whether we physically go or not, we bear the responsibility to properly expend the resources in our care.

When studying, ask many questions. A people's identity is tightly woven into their expression of culture. What are the language, arts, and social traditions? What are the religious practices? What festivals and celebrations create the rhythm of the community? What are the leadership structure and political organization? Does the community have a turbulent history? What chronic problems do the people struggle with? Each response is a window into the wants and needs of the community, offering insight into "unknown-god" concepts like the one the apostle Paul discovered in Athens (Acts 17:16-34).

Potential pitfalls lurk when we underestimate or ignore the social complexities. Many challenges exist in communities of developing countries. Some missionaries place education for local children as one of their primary ministry goals. While the goal of educating the next generation is laudable, Gary Haugen and Victor Boutros document the futility of building schools in violence-ridden locales. If a young girl might be violated on her way to school, parents would not allow her to attend. When criminals operate with impunity, they minimize the potential benefit of community-development initiatives. As we identify the obstacles for ministry, we more wisely craft a strategy.

Often the complexity leads us to form partnerships for interdisciplinary approaches. Specialized organizations can bring knowledge and abilities to address complicated needs. Recognizing the relationship between effective justice systems and impoverished communities led our church to partner with both local missionaries and International Justice Mission (IJM) in Guatemala. The IJM office works alongside the Guatemalan justice system to reduce child sexual exploitation. From the police officers to the judges, they strive for whole-country transformation. As IJM and their government partners work to reduce crime and corruption, missionaries are better able to focus on the spiritual and educational needs of children and families.

Know your travel companions. The next step in developing a missions strategy is to create a snapshot of your congregation. The continuums shape the model for missional engagement, but the church family provides the means for action. The expression of mission will look different for every church and every person. The men, women, and children who make up the local church bring the unique gifts, talents, and passions to serve. When we examine our own church composition, interaction with mission partners improves dramatically. For example, if your congregation is passionate about football or baseball, consider supporting a sports ministry to reach local children with the gospel. Connection with the mission will come naturally for church members.

Survey your congregation to learn their gifts, talents, and passions. A paper survey at the end of a worship service or an online version emailed during the week will provide valuable insights. The responses will summarize the passions of congregation members and will be well worth your time. There are numerous tools available to help with surveying.

Another gauge of your congregation's missional interests is their participation in previous outreaches. The Holy Spirit prompts and mobilizes as needs arise. When efforts touch the hearts and minds of congregants, they are especially generous. What drew the most support from members? What received few contributions? Did the collection for school supplies for impoverished children draw an abundance of donations? Did the request for canned goods fill the church lobby with hundreds of pounds of food? Did the special collection for planting churches in southeast Asia receive funds far beyond expectations? Congregants want to make a difference. The influence of the church expands as they connect and contribute. "Each of you should use whatever gift you have received to serve others, as faithful stewards of God's grace in its various forms" (1 Peter 4:10). We mobilize the congregation to use their abilities for God's glory.

Fellow missions leaders are also travel companions in the journey toward excellence in missional engagement. Connections through mission networks benefit both leaders and the church. The exchange of ideas and best practices is well worth the investment of time. If a network does not exist in your area, connect with missions leaders at other churches and create one. National and international networks of churches, mission agencies, denominations, and missiologists also exist to connect and share resources. Missio Nexus is the oldest and largest network, bringing hundreds of missions leaders together to mobilize expertise for global collaboration. Additional nondenominational networks, such as visionSynergy, Sixteen:Fifteen Missions, and VERGE, also work to equip church leaders to discern God's global mission.

Plan the route. Third, as you calculate your route, several possibilities will present themselves. Some roads will lead to deeper connection with current missionaries while others may lead to dead ends and the termination of a mission partnership. Other routes may lead to collaboration with a new partner or even the development of a new ministry. You are now ready to turn theory into an action plan.

If your research results in a compass bearing that points toward one or more of your current mission partners, discover how to increase connections with them. Talk with them about their greatest needs and their vision for the community. Missionaries appreciate opportunities to connect resources of support churches with the needs in the field. Encourage congregants also to connect with missionaries online. Robert Lupton described best missions practices for a church as those that will "raise their members' awareness to the needs, help connect them to opportunities, and let God do the rest."

One mission partner told me, "I don't want to just be a push pin on a church's bulletin board." Not many of us have cork boards with maps anymore, but I understood his desire to be more than a two-dimensional face of missions. Church websites can provide links to their missionaries' personal blogs and electronic newsletters and direct people to updates offered via Instagram, Facebook, Twitter, YouTube, Vimeo, or other social media outlets.

When planning one route for our congregation, we recognized the Lord calling us to a relationship-based, sustainable ministry with vulnerable children. Several families foster children or are adoptive parents.

Many members sponsor children through parachurch organizations. Special collections for children's needs (school supplies for children in the local shelter, coats for an elementary school, support for orphans in Zambia) draw tremendous responses. So we began investing more with our mission partners who brought justice and mercy into the lives of lost and abandoned children. Congregation members continue to join our teams to mentor in the local school as well as to serve onsite with international partners.

As you examine possible routes, you may find it is time to end a mission partnership. Your assessments may reveal a new direction for your church's missions funds. A newly found calling to an unreached people group or a business-as-mission initiative may require a realignment of funding. Alternatively, a missionary's change in focus may not align with your strategic plan. One church ended a long-time partnership with a missionary when he left his campus ministry position to plant a church. The supporting church was not opposed to church planting, but their calling to young adults drew them to seek another collegiate partner instead.

If you plan to discontinue support, communicate with the missionary as soon as possible. Be wise, compassionate, and merciful. Explain the reasons for ending the partnership. In my experience, missionaries have responded with gracious thanksgiving for the previous years of support and with understanding for the church's strategic decision. We all prayerfully trust the Lord to provide resources for their continued work. If possible, consider spreading out the reduction of financial support over several years. For example, decrease next year's funding by one third, another third the following year, then the next year funding ceases.

Your discussions may reveal gifts and abilities of your congregation to meet a specific unmet need. Toward the strategic goal to reduce local poverty, for example, my church recognized the difficulties low-income neighbors experienced in eating healthy meals. The expense of fresh food was cost prohibitive. So, under the expertise of one church member, we planted a vegetable garden on the church property. If the Lord stirs the desire to develop a new ministry, share the idea with your church family and willingly receive their suggestions. Additional prayer and discussion will help shape your prospective ministry plan.

Often a significant investment of time and funding is needed to start a new ministry. In this initial stage, however, grace is also needed as methods are tried and adjusted to see what fits best. One way to launch a new ministry is to begin with a pilot project. With a clear description of the work and a definitive time commitment, invite church and community members into the venture. Begin small, then evaluate. In *The New Conspirators*, Tom Sine writes about the ways God is prompting new missional expressions one mustard seed at a time. From improved education in Hoboken, New Jersey to rural agricultural cooperatives, he explores missional engagement in the twenty-first-century church. Sine highlights entrepreneurs who are reimagining ways to connect resources with the needs of others. When we unleash creativity and join God on mission, lives change and communities transform.

Your church may also send new missionaries. Responsibility for their care before, during, and after their service is critical for their effectiveness in the field and beyond. A partnership with a mission-sending agency may provide the best support for your potential missionary. Prayerfully work together to help members discern their call and how it aligns with your church's missions strategy. Many agencies recommend enrollment in the *Perspectives on the World Christian Movement* class as a first step in a parishioner's discernment process. Available online and in many local venues, *Perspectives* offers people the opportunity to explore biblical foundations for missions, historical contexts, international cultures, and personal responses to God's call to make his name known in all the nations.

Your call to missions may also lead to a new partnership. If passion for serving people experiencing homelessness arises, for example, investigate existing initiatives in your community. Partnering with an organization actively addressing the issue may be the most effective means to serve. Meet with their staff to find out more about their work. Then, instead of creating a duplicate effort, look for ways to serve together and build on the work in progress. Mission organizations such as The Outreach Foundation consult with churches to help connect ministry involvement with long-term relationships.

Partnerships create the critical accountability and collaboration that solo ministry lacks. When drawing on a larger collection of talents and resources, the body of Christ mobilizes more effectively. Missions strategist Phill Butler asserts that joint ventures are the only remaining alternative for the church to move forward with effective missional engagement.

> There needs to be a radical and broad new level of commitment to common working, acknowledging that effectively addressing challenges such as the fulfillment of the Great Commission can only be done collaboratively. In response, ministry leadership, field personnel, Boards of Trustees, and kingdom investors need strongly to affirm, support, and engage in practical collective action.

No era has ever seen the crisscrossing of missionaries we are experiencing today: "The 21st century has witnessed the sending of international missionaries to all the world's countries from almost every country." Reversing the pattern of the last century, three countries in the Global South are among the top-ten missionary-sending countries. The opportunity to form ministry networks is unprecedented. With mission-minded neighbors from many different cultures and countries, we merely need to reach out and explore options. Globalization is allowing the proliferation of partnerships between Western and non-Western schools, agencies, and churches in everything from strategies to missionary education.

Another benefit to partnerships is their protection against a myopic view of God's global mission. The interdependence within the body of Christ reminds us of the broader kingdom. Accountability, financial backing, and shared resources improve the efficiency and the potential for favorable kingdom outcomes. We need one another in order to be the most effective witnesses for Christ in our local communities and to the ends of the earth. As the saying goes, "If you want to go fast, go alone. If you want to go far, go together."

A networked, global church has stunning potential. Our worldwide "corporation" manages tremendous resources. Our people, financial assets, property holdings, and expertise rival any Fortune 500 company. Connecting the local branches is the next step in our global work to advance the gospel. Partnerships reduce redundancy while expanding influence. As trust builds, initiatives grow. The best partners enhance each other's strengths and complement each other's weaknesses. Interdependency brings a unity that is pleasing to God. Therefore, as you prepare your missions strategy, consider adopting a sister church in an impoverished community, partnering with a local school, or starting a collaborative venture with business entrepreneurs to reach an unengaged people group.

REVISITING OUR STRATEGIES

Your missions strategy is never truly done. Because we live in an ever-changing world, we need to reassess our missions strategies regularly. Prayer and continued conversation open the way to discovering God's ongoing plan. He is ever on the move and we remain under the leadership of his Spirit. People, situations, and culture are also in a constant state of change. Your awareness and reassessment will ensure the relevance of your strategic plan. Be open to altering methods and ministry as necessary. As a community recovers from a disaster, for example, the goal is to help them move toward sustainability. A prolonged crisis-response strategy causes more harm than good in long-term development.

A wealthy suburban church served regularly in an impoverished town in Kentucky. Their goal of community transformation progressed over the years. Visiting teams hosted children's ministry events, completed home repairs, donated gently used clothes, and raised funds for school repairs. Relationships grew as they connected with local churches, the community-center staff, and many of the town's leaders. As the region experienced economic depression, the suburban church was able to offer many resources.

But the church's involvement came to an abrupt halt during one of their construction trips. A town member casually mentioned that she was glad the summer mission team had finally arrived. She said that they rely on the visiting church to clean the park each year, and that this year the clean-up included removal of a collapsing shed, which looked horrible. She explained that the town made sure to have work for the team each year. The suburban church had created an unintentional dependency. They had succeeded in building relationships but long-term development was stalled.

We need to check our compass bearing frequently to confirm that our direction remains true to our initial calling. As time passes and we become familiar with the terrain, we are tempted to set the compass aside. But when we do this our kingdom-focused navigation gets off track. The original intent of a partnership may have been strategic, but gradually the calendar becomes the driving force. Activities that aim to reduce local poverty become routine and the church loses its burden for building relationships. It's Thanksgiving: time to do food. It's Christmas: time to collect gifts for needy children.

During my orienteering days, at least one team in every race suffered from the influence of a flashlight or a key chain. Metal objects distort the compass reading. Not realizing they were on a magnetically altered course, the errant team wandered far from the intended destination point. Continual review of a missions strategy helps identify distractions and their unintended influences. When we maintain our compass bearing, our steps remain kingdom oriented. We can more quickly adjust, thereby reducing potential for harm.

Influences that threaten to send us in the wrong direction include distorting biblical principles, spiritual hoarding, addiction to experiences, obsession with results, and loss of passion.

First, missional engagement is based on three biblical principles: glorify God, obey his precepts, and meet the needs of others. When our ministry narrows to only one of the three principles, our view of missions becomes distorted. For example, the focus on meeting physical needs alone overlooks the power of the gospel for healing and reconciliation. The church is more than a group of goodwill ambassadors from a faith-based organization. On the other hand, when obedience is elevated, rules begin to hinder instead of providing valuable parameters for ministry. Attempts to build rigid, step-by-step models create tension in situations that require a more flexible approach.

Second, spiritual hoarding can be a temptation. God assembles the talents and resources of people into local churches for use in his kingdom. The number of abilities and assets, including buildings and vehicles, that we have is staggering. But management and care of these gifts can distract us from their intended use: bank accounts grow large, faith grows stale, the church turns its focus inward. We must not hoard our resources or lose sight of their purpose to mobilize the church for mission.

Third, the prevailing culture of travel and hands-on adventure can create more harm than good. When experiences drive our decisions, the needs of the mission field are undervalued and even discounted. Some congregants wait all year for the next short-term mission project, not for the serving opportunity but for the anticipated "spiritual high" and travel experience. Awareness of our addiction will deter it from distorting missional engagement.

Fourth, we can become too focused on seeing results. In our haste toward accomplishing goals, we tend to abandon efforts too early. Kingdom work involves breakthroughs in the unseen world. Human eyes lack the ability to observe spiritual battles and incremental heart transformation. Five-year plans and annual objectives can be at odds with God's eternal frame of reference. Metrics and goals are valuable, but they can also distort our compass.

Finally, the trappings of daily routine can erode our sense of calling. Repetition leads to loss of passion. Everything feels ordinary. In this giant world of brokenness and pain, our simple acts of service—ongoing conversation with an agnostic neighbor or dropping off another hot casserole—sometimes feel insignificant. We may need the admonishment that John spoke to the church at Ephesus: "I know your deeds, your hard work. . . .

You have persevered and have endured hardships for my name, and have not grown weary. Yet I hold this against you: You have forsaken the love you had at first" (Revelation 2:2-4). Each selfless act reflects God, radiating his goodness amid the darkness. When light pierces the darkness, angels rejoice and darkness is overcome.

OUR CALL TO GO

It was 1979. Our youth group of twenty sat on a collection of stumps and rocks in an amoeboid circle. We had set up tents earlier and would be camping for the night. Two guys tended the fire, adding enough logs for it easily to burn into next week. Our youth group leaders, Nick and Tracy, passed out copies of the *Dove Songbook*. The dancing flames drew me in until I felt a poke and was handed the stack of songbooks. Take one and pass it on.

The fire crackled and pine sap popped. The intermittent breeze altered the flow of smoke and it drifted toward my spot in the circle.

Through the haze I saw Nick reach for his guitar and enter his private music bubble of plunking strings. He winced with each out-of-tune twang. More plucking. More knob tightening and loosening. A slight nod. Next string. Finally, with a broad smile and toss of his long blond curls, he strummed a satisfied finale to his tuning work.

"Let's begin with prayer, then pick out some songs." Nick balanced the songbook on his knee and the C chord launched our worship under the stars.

We sang verse after verse of camp songs.

Then came the song that changed everything. I had sung it dozens of times before, but somehow that night the lyrics of "Pass It On" took hold of my heart. I did indeed want to tell the gospel message from the mountain tops. I wanted the world to know. The folk-guitar music inspired by Matthew 28:19-20 caused the living Word to leap from the pages of my King James Bible and find a permanent home in my heart. The Holy Spirit ignited a spark within me that would drive my desire to seek out the poor, the lonely, and the lost for the rest of my days.

While all believers are called to go, God calls each of us in different ways. Some missionary friends felt his Spirit beckon through testimonies at a missions conference, others through a sermon that unexpectedly put the desire in their heart. Scripture records the Lord calling people to missions through dreams, visions, prophets, a burning bush, and even a talking donkey. As uniquely as he made us, he likewise tailors his revelations. Regardless of how the calling comes, may we each respond as Isaiah did, "Here am I. Send me!" (Isaiah 6:8).

Although directions vary, our travels can be purposeful and Christ-centered when we are equipped with a compass to serve. With a navigational bearing set, the journey can begin. But to begin we must take the first step—and that by far is the most difficult one. In C. S. Lewis's *Screwtape Letters,* a senior demon offers advice to a junior demon on how to interfere in the spiritual life of humans: "The great thing is to prevent his doing anything. . . . Let him do anything but act. No amount of piety in his imagination and affections will harm us if we can keep it out of his will." May it never be so! With a strategy in hand, let's step out to serve.

As tangible expressions of God's love and presence, our lives acquire new meaning. The arms swinging hammers and sawing boards are answers to prayer for the young family whose Appalachian home is falling apart. The voice sharing the gospel in an urban shanty town answers a woman's silent plea for significance. Hours donated by the local dentist answer the prayer of the homeless man with an abscessed tooth. Here in real life we experience loving others as Jesus taught. As we align our missions strategy with effective practice, the watching world observes the one true God. We serve to draw others into a reconciled relationship with him.

As we extend our attention beyond our own culture and community, we discover the stunning breadth of human existence across our planet. Appreciating different cultures, whether of diaspora people groups in our own community or villages far away, expands our understanding of the family of God. We find beloved brothers and sisters in the worship service of a Costa Rican church with its dirt floor and worn plastic patio chairs.

We learn from one another and relationships form. Together we share the name of Jesus with all who have not yet heard. We go with confidence and the power of the Holy Spirit. Although God could have chosen angels or Jesus himself, he now calls us to be his kingdom laborers.

Friends, the harvest is plentiful. Let's pick up our compasses and travel well into his harvest fields.

QUESTIONS

1. How would you assess the needs in your community? What government offices, agencies, or nonprofit organizations would offer insights? What online sources would you consult to assist your research?

2. How would you create a snapshot of the gifts and abilities of your congregation? Brainstorm the possibilities. (For instance, would you design an online survey and/or distribute a questionnaire at the end of a worship service? Would you gather focus groups for discussion?)

3. With your gifts, passions, and calling, how would you take the gospel message to the nations if you had access to all resources? Imagine the possibilities without constraints.

4. Compare your compass bearing in each of the seven conversations with your ministry partners. How effective are your current missional engagements in fulfilling God's call in your life? In the life of your congregation?

5. Given the complexity of missional engagement, what benefits do you think a missions strategy would provide for your congregation?

ACKNOWLEDGMENTS

I thank God for my family. Without their support this book would be nonexistent. Many thanks to my husband, Chris, who endured countless tumbleweeds of dust rolling across unvacuumed floors and far too many nights of international buffet (i.e., leftovers). I love you with all my heart and am grateful to be on this journey with you.

Thank you to my children—Elise, Aaron, and daughter-in-law Rachel. Your patience was legendary as I disappeared daily behind my keyboard. I appreciate your encouraging words as this book took shape over the months—the many, many months. You bless my life in more ways than I can express and I look forward to many more adventures with you.

I remain indebted to my parents, Ron and Judy Recher. My childhood experiences of traveling and camping inspired a profound awe of God's creation. Gazing out the back seat car window, I watched miles and miles of stunning terrain pass. Thank you for always encouraging new interests, from art lessons to horse ownership! I appreciate your sacrifices and your constant love for Lisa, Randy, and me.

Thank you to my prayer partners Nancy Anthony and Elizabeth Luffy. You have been caregivers of my soul in all the joys and challenges of integrating faith, life, and writing. I thank God for the amazing women of the

Redbud Writers Guild. Your counsel, experience, and generosity paved my road to publication. Thank you for holding me accountable and for prompting each step along the way.

Many thanks to the readers of the first manuscript drafts. Your selfless hours improved the book countless times over: Maureen Erickson, Beth Ernest, Aaron Gordon, Jenny Gordon, Dorothy Greco, Erin Hawley, Austin House, Alan MacDonald, Janna Northrup, Afton Rorvik, Margot Starbuck, and Leslie Verner. Thank you to Leslie Leyland Fields and my Alaskan Harvester Island Workshop friends who also helped formulate this book. I thank God also for Terri Kraus—her confidence in me inspired my work toward professional writing.

Thank you to my church family at Centreville Presbyterian. I'm grateful for your patience while I was writing, your willingness to listen to my meandering thoughts, and your heart to serve the community and beyond. You challenge me to always seek the best paths for our missional engagement.

Thank you to Paul Borthwick for writing the foreword. I have long been a reader of his books and articles. Dr. Borthwick's *Organizing Your Youth Ministry* was one of my first purchases when I joined a church staff in 1994. I am immensely grateful for his time to support my book. Sharing the cover of *Mapping Church Missions* with him lends credibility that I know will encourage potential readers to explore the book.

I am indebted to those who helped craft this book. My editors at Inter-Varsity Press, Ethan McCarthy and Anna Gissing, pushed me into greater depths with each chapter. Every conversation, suggestion, and revision prompted more insightful paragraphs. Thank you, Ethan, for the repeated nudges into nuanced meanings and undercurrents. Really. Many thanks to copyeditor and stunning word master Kristie Berglund. Her expertise smoothed, clarified, and created a more coherent book. Huge shout-out to InterVarsity Press art director David Fassett for his creative cover design. Thank you for visually capturing the content of the book, expertly building in multilayered and intriguing detail.

Thank you to my agent Dan Balow at the Steve Laube Agency for his support and advice throughout this publication journey. I am grateful for your wisdom and expertise.

Finally, thank you to all who allowed me to share their stories. Your willingness to be part of this book allows all of us to continue to learn and grow.

> The Lord bless you [all]
> and keep you;
> the Lord make his face shine on you
> and be gracious to you;
> the Lord turn his face toward you
> and give you peace. (Numbers 6:24-26)

APPENDIX 1: BEYOND "MINUTE FOR MISSIONS"

CONNECTING CONGREGATIONS WITH MISSION PARTNERS

As missions leaders we develop relationships with our mission partners and connect our congregations with them and their work. This can be a challenging task given the many responsibilities and activities happening in the lives of our church families. What are some creative ways to increase meaningful involvement in missions?

CREATE A VARIETY OF WAYS TO CONNECT

Congregants have a wide range of financial and time availability. But whether single parents or senior citizens, people want to serve. To best engage them, offer various options of involvement. Talk with mission partners about various ways to serve them and to serve the people in their ministry location. Not only will the variety provide a way to explore the callings of church members, the range of opportunities also allows your members to deepen their connection with mission partners in ways natural to them. Variety may be available in length of time commitment, location, gifts, abilities, and interests.

Time. Offer numerous time commitments: one hour (shop for food pantry, drive a meal to a homebound person, pray for and write an encouraging note to a missionary); several hours weekly (serve breakfast at a homeless shelter, visit a sick neighbor, mentor a child); a week (serve on a crosscultural mission team, complete a project at a local ministry building such as paint a room or spring clean their kitchen).

Location. Develop ways to serve from various locations: home (letter writing, phone calls, computer work, advocacy), local (connect congregants with needs in the community such as shelters, transitional homes, and schools), regional (organize weekend or weeklong teams to serve partners within driving distance), international (coordinate opportunities to serve in places where passports are required).

Gifts and abilities. Offer opportunities to explore use of gifts and talents for kingdom purposes: teaching (such as children's ministry, financial planning, job-readiness programs), administration (office skills, computer work, newsletter editor), leadership (organize new initiatives, facilitate community work day, research new ministry partnerships). Mobilize people to use their skills in construction, painting, photography, gardening, music, and so on.

Interests. Organize mission partners thematically to help congregants match their passions with purpose. An impact area of *children and families* could include mission partners focused on orphan care, local schools, and mentoring at-risk teens. An impact area of *poverty and homelessness* could include partnerships with home rehabs, job programs, and food pantries. An *evangelism* impact area could include church planting, developing missionaries, and supporting missions to unreached people groups. Congregants who know their areas of interest will be able to browse mission options more efficiently.

Finances. Share a wide range of ways to support mission partners financially. Congregants can be monthly supporters of a missionary, sponsor a child, donate funds to purchase items for a ministry (such as gloves and

socks for neighbors experiencing homelessness), or make special donations to a mission partner's new initiative.

BE INTENTIONAL AND COMMUNICATIVE

Define the needs and commitment clearly. It's helpful to create simple job
descriptions that outline expectations and length of service, especially for
ministry commitments that can be ongoing. At the end of the commitment
period, intentionally release people from their ministry. Those who genuinely desire to continue can recommit to serve another term, while those
who are ready to resign can explore other opportunities without guilt
or burnout.

Keep everyone well informed. Send emails (brief and descriptive), hang
up signs and posters about new opportunities, maintain links to missionaries on your website, develop a team to help communicate through social
media, give verbal announcements on Sunday mornings, utilize video testimonies from church members and missionaries, send regular electronic
or paper newsletters. Continually hold your mission partners before your
church family.

DEVELOP NEXT STEPS

Follow up with congregants as they serve. When people step into their
calling, they often want to pursue further connections with ministry
partners. They may hesitate to offer their time and abilities to your partners
but would be willing to consider the possibilities with you. Over coffee ask
how they sense the Lord leading them to further engage. Be prepared to
suggest next steps, offer training, and explore opportunities.

A congregant exploring missions may begin by donating a dozen or-
anges to a soup kitchen. Then the next month he might bring a hot casserole. Next he might commit to the monthly rotation to serve breakfast.
Then maybe he joins their social media team to raise awareness about local
poverty. As his investment in the ministry grows, relationships form. A
next step for him could be to lead the shelter's weekly Bible study or

manage the volunteer team. From adding an item to a grocery list to weekly engagement, our congregants soon discover various ways to use their gifts and talents for God's kingdom work and encourage others to do the same.

APPENDIX 2:
SCENARIOS FOR
FURTHER REFLECTION

This book's seven conversations introduce us to the plethora of directions available on God's compass of engagement. The conversations isolate factors that impact our missions strategy, including intentional choices as well as subconscious preferences. The complexities of missions and partnerships require assessment across all issues at all times.

To move beyond an academic discussion of continuums, this appendix offers three practical scenarios to foster further reflection. Each scenario explores a different role of engagement with missions. The stories are fictional compilations of real situations. Place yourself in each scene to clarify your passion for missions, your hopes for the church, and your call to serve. Questions follow each scenario to help distinguish between the continuums and promote ongoing conversation.

SCENARIO 1: JOE McMILLAN'S HEART
FOR COMMUNITY INVOLVEMENT

He closed the car door. The silence wrapped him like a familiar couch blanket. Helping at the homeless shelter had sucked every ounce of energy from his body.

Today was no different than the previous three visits. That morning, as he prepared to go, Joe thought it would be different this time. But once again he found himself watching the clock, waiting for his final hour. As soon as his three-hour commitment concluded, he said polite goodbyes and left.

Since his retirement from the Federal Highway Administration, Joe has been in search of ways to serve in the community. The homeless shelter was his latest attempt. His church has a long-time partnership with the ministry. At-risk men and women find safety and the tangible presence of God in a dedicated staff, both paid and volunteer. Many people have stepped onto a path of recovery and healing in their care.

But it was not the place for Joe.

That evening the shelter experience came up in conversation with his wife, Martha.

"We'll keep praying, Joe. You'll find a place to serve."

"Bottom line is, I don't know what to say to them." Joe reached for another tomato to chop for the dinner salad. "The homeless guests' lives are so different from mine."

"What about teaching one of the lunchtime Bible studies at the shelter?" Martha had seen her husband pull several dysfunctional government offices together. Leadership and teaching were clearly his gifts.

"I don't think so. My knowledge of the Bible is too limited. Teaching, yes, I like. But not when I don't know the subject well enough."

Joe tossed the salad. Martha stirred the spaghetti sauce and checked on the noodles.

"Paul called. He asked me to help with the next Habitat for Humanity house."

"Great idea! You've been wanting to do a hands-on project." Martha pulled plates out of the cabinet. "I'm on their email list and get weekly notices of their volunteer needs."

"I told him I could help on their demolition days. But I don't know how to do skilled jobs like hanging drywall, laying carpet, and certainly not electrical or plumbing work."

"I'm sure there will be other things to do, Joe. Just give it a chance."

"I will. How did things go at the school today?"

"Great! I love mentoring the children. We did double-digit addition and subtraction. Even I can still do second-grade math! I'm going back to-morrow to help the reading specialists reorganize their bookshelves." Martha's eyes sparkled when she talked about volunteering at the school.

"I'm sure they love having you." Joe placed napkins and silverware on the table.

"Being at the school every week lets me meet more people in our neighborhood. I can even talk about faith occasionally. One of the teachers asked me to pray for her dad. He was recently diagnosed with cancer. We talked about God's presence and his hand in healing. It's also been a great way to get to know our own church family better. Seven other members are part of the mentoring team." Martha paused. "Maybe you . . ."

"No. Don't even go there, Martha." Joe tipped his chin down and looked over the top of his eyeglasses. "You know I am not good with children. They need about fifteen or sixteen more years of life before I can actually converse with them."

Martha smirked and gave him a gentle push. "Okay. Let's eat. But we will find ways that you can connect in the community."

The weeks moved along. Habitat for Humanity received all the permits and paperwork needed to begin the new home rehab.

Prayer and introductions kicked off the first day's work.

"Thank you, Pastor Reyes, for your prayer as we begin work this morning." The site leader, Theo, pulled on his work gloves. "Our plan today is to remove the kitchen cabinets and counters. They're unusable because of water damage. We'll also tear out the drywall in the dining room and family room."

Paul sipped coffee from his thermal mug. "Joe, want to start in the family room with me?"

"Sure. Let's do it!"

The morning flew by. Hacksaws whirred to life. Drywall ripped. Voices called out instruction. Discarded cabinets crashed into the dumpster in the driveway. Grunts and laughter erupted with equal regularity.

At noon a family from a local church brought lunch for the whole crew. They spread out a feast of sandwiches, deviled eggs, bags of chips, and sweet tea on the makeshift table of sawhorses and plywood.

"We're making good progress." Paul spoke through his mouthful of turkey sandwich.

"The dumpster is filling fast." Joe sat with a satisfying moan. "It feels good to take a break."

"We'll finish the family room this afternoon. I'm concerned about the front corner near the foyer. The subflooring has water damage. It may extend into the foyer. I don't think they used exterior-grade plywood in the original construction."

"Want to pull up the rotten wood this afternoon?"

"No, we'll stay on the wallboard and carpet removal." Paul somehow managed to fit the rest of the sandwich in his mouth. "The unexpected always turns up in these rehabs. Never know what we'll find. We'll tell Theo so he can add it to the pending work list."

"Okay, you're the boss." Joe stretched his back and neck. The physical work felt good.

By Friday, though, his body did not enjoy the labor so much. More ibuprofen. More time getting ready. Then he was finally out the door for the final day of demo week.

"I'm not a young man anymore," he had lamented to Martha the previous evening. "I take more breaks than the other volunteers on the site.

They keep telling me it's fine. But I'm not comfortable sitting while everyone else is working."

Martha listened with her usual patience. "Maybe you could be more of a site leader? You are so good at seeing the big picture and breaking down the tasks needed to get there."

"Not when it comes to construction. Yes, I know our end goal. But the world of galvanized nails, drywall measurements, and two-by-fours is foreign to me." Joe turned his shoulders left to crack his back.

"Ugh . . . stop doing that, Joe!"

"I'm fine!" Relief washed over Joe's face with the cacophony of snap-crackle-pops. "It's been good helping this week but next week requires more skilled work. I don't plan to continue with the house. I told Paul I'd be happy to help when they have another demo job."

"I believe they do two or three houses a year."

Joe nodded. "By the way, have you heard of Jobs for Life?"

"No, I haven't. What is it?"

"Pastor Jeff came by the Habitat site yesterday and was talking about it. It's a faith-based course that helps people stuck in poverty to move toward better employment opportunities. The curriculum sounds quite comprehensive. He said it addresses dignity of work, vocational planning, roadblocks, and more."

"Sounds like all the stuff you used to teach your new hires."

"Yes, but with a Christ-centeredness I couldn't include." Joe continued. "From helping in the shelter, I know giving food, assisting with rent, and other emergency services are needed in our community. But I have wondered what we could do to help encourage people take the next steps toward long-term progress."

Martha nodded. Joe had expressed these concerns many times.

"What you're suggesting, though, would take a longer commitment. It's really walking alongside people for months, even years."

"You're right, and I have that kind of time now. Apparently, our church is going to host a Jobs for Life class in the fall. They need mentors, teachers, and site coordinators." Joe paused. "I think I'll go to the information meeting next week."

QUESTIONS

1. List the continuums represented in this scenario. Describe where Joe's and Martha's compass bearings point on the continuums.

2. With whom do you most identify in this scenario? Share similarities and differences with your compass bearing for missional engagement.

3. How would you counsel Joe in his next steps? What additional ways could the pastor assist Joe in his search?

4. How would you develop strategies to help congregants connect with ministries in your community?

SCENARIO 2: THE STEWARTS' CALL TO THE MISSION FIELD

"Thank you for returning my call. I appreciate the clarification and we'll get back to you soon." Maria hung up the phone and turned to Nick with a grin that reached her eyes.

"So, did they suggest healthcare options?" Nick asked about the latest concern in their research of mission agencies.

"Yes, they have a couple different plans. I liked that they also have crisis care and counseling partners available within their network." Maria poured two mugs of coffee.

"Sounds like great resources, but it took them three weeks and several emails to respond to one simple question." Mike reached for his laptop. "Being in the same denomination I don't have any theological concerns, but I am disappointed with their lack of communication. I'm also confused by their complicated organizational structure."

"Yes, but their connections with so many networks provide resources that the two smaller sending agencies don't have." Maria settled into the kitchen chair next to her husband and handed him a mug.

"True. And their initial screening and training processes are quite comprehensive." Nick opened the browser tab with all their bookmarked mission organizations. "However, I don't believe they offer the spiritual direction and leadership development the other two agencies do."

Last year Nick and Maria had met with their pastor when they first sensed a new direction for their lives. Encouraged in their discussions, they began praying about next steps. Several months ago, they formally entered a period of discernment to explore God's call to the mission field.

"But if we really feel called to the Middle East, neither of the smaller agencies have much of a presence there." Maria sipped her coffee.

"No, but International Care includes the region as a high priority goal in their ministry expansion. Plus, their member care representative has been very responsive to our questions." Nick opened the "2020 Goals" page on the International Care website.

"I loved meeting their South American partners last week. The camaraderie among them speaks volumes about their agency. Nick, maybe the Lord is calling us to help expand their Middle Eastern presence."

"Maybe so. If we could identify a specific place to serve, then we would be able to research communities and find local partners. Your Arabic language skills would be critical to talking with the local outreaches already on the ground."

Nick clicked the "Next Steps" page. Together they scrolled down the list. Interview. Psychological exam. Pastoral recommendation. Peer references. Exploratory course. Support raising. Goal setting workshop. Conflict mediation class.

"This process is long and complicated." The chair groaned as Maria leaned back. "It could take a year or more just to raise the financial support."

"We need to keep praying."

Weeks passed as Maria and Nick immersed themselves in Scripture and prayer. The conversations, phone calls, and emails continued.

Late one evening as the couple discussed the reality of leaving their jobs and stepping into full-time ministry, they experienced a profound sense of God's peace and presence. It was time.

"Maria, I'm ready to commit." A quick nod punctuated Nick's decision. Without hesitation, Maria responded. "I am too! Amen!"

Their Bible study that evening had stirred their hearts and prompted their final step into full-time missions. Now what? Nick's mind worked like his software-development job: systematic and deliberate. All good but problematic when heading in a direction where all the answers did not exist.

"The people of the Middle East continue to burden me." Nick continued but his eyes focused on some place far off in the distance. "I've been thinking . . ."

Maria knew that look. It always preceded Nick's statements of calculated risk and a mindset shift.

"With all the damaged infrastructure in Syria and Iraq, maybe the Lord would have me use my computer knowledge toward a very practical need."

"Go on . . ." Maria leaned forward.

"I know we shifted our prayer focus to North Africa and even the refugee communities in southern Europe, but what if we joined the work to expand International Care's internet cafe and ESL school in Lebanon's refugee camps? We could expand their courses to include computer skills."

"Ooh, yes! I noticed on their website how much the enrollment in the ESL classes is growing. The program director mentioned in one of the articles that they are receiving requests to learn computer skills. You would be so good at teaching that! Then maybe I could use my accounting experience to help manage the financial side of the business. But . . . this is not the evangelism focus I thought we wanted."

"It would indeed be a major shift in our thinking." Nick began pacing the kitchen. "Our primary goal though would remain to draw people to Jesus. But instead of learning church-planting strategies, we would focus on influence through education and excellence in business practices."

"We would have to work hard to show potential supporters how business development can be a viable platform for missions." Maria joined in the pacing. "We will need to be clear how the gospel is woven through the business in the services offered and in student-teacher relationships."

"Plus, when students return to Syria and Iraq, they can have a profound influence in rebuilding their countries by using new computer skills." Nick stopped. His next words stilled the air with a determination and purpose he had not felt in a long time. "As we form friendships, we will find opportunities for spiritual conversations. Our students will learn about Jesus and, Lord willing, take the gospel message to family and friends when they can return home."

QUESTIONS

1. List the continuums represented in this scenario. Describe where Maria's and Nick's compass bearings point on the continuums.

2. How would you counsel Maria and Nick in their next steps? What additional ways could the church come alongside them in their search?

3. How would you develop strategies to help congregants discern a call to crosscultural missions?

SCENARIO 3: THE MISSIONS COMMITTEE MEETING

They sat in a beige classroom in the church building. The air, still and sterile, felt warm.

"If we reduce our funding to the Ozark Building Project, we would be able to support Luis Rivera's work with the Honduran children living in the garbage dump." The green cushion on Brenda's padded metal chair did little to reduce her discomfort with the meeting, now moving into its second hour. As the chairperson, she helped guide the missions committee to coordinate outreaches and provide oversight for the church's ministry partners.

"Our long-term partnership and support of the OBP is not something we can reduce." Ken tapped his pen and leafed through the proposals again. "But I do believe we need to consider how to further support the Harvest Reach agency. Demands on their food pantry continue to increase."

"OBP is doing fine, Ken. According to their Annual Report, they are well funded. It's time to consider how we can impact the desperately poor slums in these Central American countries." Brenda struggled with Ken's goal of increased involvement with the local community at the expense of global outreach.

Lucy cleared her throat. "But I also believe our presence here in town is important. I'm interested in everyone's thoughts on the Harvest Reach food pantry. What do you think of their new name and branding? They are transitioning to the name 'H & R' and are moving away from their Christian roots. Because they no longer share the gospel with clients, I actually want to propose a reduction in our funding for them."

"But H & R continues to include a declaration of Christian faith in their mission and vision statements," Brenda offered.

"Many of our members are able to volunteer with H & R because they are local. How many people would actually fly to Honduras to work with Luis Rivera's ministry?" Ken pushed back in his chair. "Also, how safe is it over there?"

"I agree that the Honduran outreach has risks." Brenda felt the heat creeping up her neck. She wondered if she was visibly red. "But don't you think Jesus cares about these children?"

"Yes, so maybe we could just take up a one-time, special offering?"

"We could show a video that explains the issue. Congregation members can make personal donations also, if they want."

"Let's add a display in the lobby for people who miss the video on Sunday." One committee member picked up the conversation as soon as another concluded.

Brenda struggled to keep up with the rapid-fire brainstorming shooting across the table.

"I'd be fine with that approach," Ken relented.

"No, wait," Brenda interrupted. "Last year we decided we would only partner with missionaries in long-term, meaningful relationships."

"Yes, but a special offering would be the perfect compromise." Lucy's calm voice drew nods around the table. "Then we could use more of our budget to supplement the expenses so more of our members can go overseas to serve our international partners."

"I disagree." It was the first time Terry had spoken the entire evening. "I am not a fan of mission trips. They are impractical, a waste of money, and are merely sanctified vacations."

"Actually, Terry, when my wife and I were missionaries in Miami, short-term teams served as a critical piece in our summer outreaches. We were able to connect with more new families after teams hosted camps than any other times of the year." Due to his years in missionary service, Brandon's voice always carried great weight.

"Hmm . . . maybe I could support more funding to send a team to a location within driving distance," Terry conceded.

And so it went for the church committee that evening. After the meeting the conversation continued.

"I had really hoped we would begin to support Rivera's work in the Honduran slums." LaVonda held the door as she and Brenda walked outside the building.

"Why didn't you say something?"

"Brenda, it was my first meeting. I was just trying to get the lay of the land. We have a lot of people with passions for different ministries."

"Yes, we do. That includes you as well." Brenda turned toward her friend. "Your heart for children reflects the concerns of many people in our congregation. Please know that I value your opinions."

"I don't know how much influence I can have." LaVonda held up the stack of papers from the meeting. "We already have so many mission partners. I have no idea who half of these people are. But apparently, we have supported some for more than a decade. How is that a partnership?"

"Exactly. Help me work with our committee to develop a strategy that reflects the unique contribution our church brings to the needs around us and around the world." Brenda's voice carried anticipation for greater things.

"I'll be back next month. I am committed to this committee for the full year. But can we meet for lunch before the next meeting? I'd appreciate some insight into each ministry partner."

QUESTIONS

1. List the continuums represented in this scenario. Describe where each committee member's (Ken, Brenda, Lucy, Terry, Brandon, La-Vonda) compass bearing points on the continuums.

2. With whom do you most identify in this scenario? Share similarities and differences with your compass bearing for missional engagement.

3. How would you counsel the committee for their next meeting? What additional information would assist their decision making?

4. How would you develop strategies to help the committee clarify their direction in missional engagement?

NOTES

INTRODUCTION: CHARTING OUR COURSE

8 *When someone behaves this way*: Kent Annan, *Slow Kingdom Coming: Practices for Doing Justice, Loving Mercy, and Walking Humbly in the World* (Downers Grove, IL: InterVarsity Press, 2016), 15-16.

9 *focus on missions reached unprecedented heights*: A. Scott Moreau, Gary Corwin, and Gary McGee, *Introducing World Missions: A Biblical, Historical, and Practical Survey* (Grand Rapids: Baker Academic, 2004), 153-54.

12 *The North American church gave over*: Todd Johnson et al., "Christianity 2015: Religious Diversity and Personal Contact," *International Bulletin of Missionary Research* 39/1 (2015): 28-29.

14 *independent mission agencies send more*: Christopher Paul Rice, "Toward a Framework for a Practical Theology of Institutions for Faith-Based Organizations" (PhD dissertation, Duke University, 2014), 25, https://dukespace.lib .duke.edu/dspace/bitstream/handle/10161/9473/Rice_divinity.duke _0066A_10027.pdf.

1 GOOD NEWS AND GOOD DEEDS

19 *Mercy is God's attitude*: Eric Swanson and Rick Rusaw, *The Externally Focused Quest: Becoming the Best Church for the Community* (San Francisco: Jossey-Bass, 2010), 156.

22 *in relating God's mission*: Ed Stetzer, "Five Reasons Missional Churches Don't Do Global Missions—And How to Fix It," *Christianity Today*, September 24, 2009, www.christianitytoday.com/edstetzer/2009/september/five-reasons -missional-churches-dont-do-global-missions.html.

23 *meeting the physical needs*: Andy Crouch, "Evangelism and Social Action: An Excerpt from *Playing God*," *Urbana Articles* (blog), December 31, 2013, https://urbana.org/blog/evangelism-and-social-action.

23   *Christian mission should not mistake*: John Rackley, "Christian Mission vs. Humanitarian Relief," *Ethics Daily* (blog), February 12, 2009, www.ethicsdaily .com/christian-mission-vs-humanitarian-relief-cms-13674.

24   *In the early to mid-1900s*: Randy Newman, "Evangelism and Social Justice," www.christianity.com/church/missions-and-evangelism/evangelism-and -social-justice.html (accessed October 19, 2017).

30   *To stay balanced*: Paul Borthwick, *Great Commission, Great Compassion: Following Jesus and Loving the World* (Downers Grove, IL: InterVarsity Press, 2013), 168.

      When we become involved: Richard Stearns, *The Hole in Our Gospel: What Does God Expect of Us? The Answer That Changed My Life and Might Just Change the World* (Nashville: Thomas Nelson, 2009), 19-20.

31   *that dimension and activity*: David Bosch, *Transforming Mission: Paradigm Shifts in Theology of Mission* (Maryknoll, NY: Orbis Books, 2011), 430.

2 NEIGHBORS NEAR AND FAR

42   *when the missional impulse is not*: Ed Stetzer, "Five Reasons Missional Churches Don't Do Global Missions—And How to Fix It," *The Exchange* (blog), September 24, 2009, www.christianitytoday.com/edstetzer/2009 /september/five-reasons-missional-churches-dont-do-global-missions .html.

42   *instead of targeting countries*: "About Dr. Winter," Ralph Winter's official website, www.ralphdwinter.org (accessed March 24, 2017).

44   *In today's globalized economy*: Michael Gryboski, "Five Trends in Christian Missions: Global Christianity Experts," *The Christian Post* (blog), May 20, 2016, www.christianpost.com/news/5-trends-in-christian-missions-global -christianity-experts-164282.

45   *In 2015 the International Mission Board*: Peggy E. Newell, *North American Mission Handbook: U.S. and Canadian Protestant Ministries Overseas* (Pasadena, CA: William Cary Library, 2017), 50.

48   *The ever-accelerating and intensifying phenomenon*: Craig Ott, "Globalization and Contextualization: Reframing the Task of Contextualization in the Twenty-First Century," *Missiology* 43/1 (2015): 44.

49   *eliminate boundaries within an organization*: Nathan Collier, "Boundary-lessness," *NSC* (blog), October 23, 2008, www.nscblog.com/miscellaneous /boundarylessness.

49   *Since boundary maintenance is a main*: Stan Nussbaum, *A Reader's Guide to Transforming Mission,* American Society of Missiology Series (New York: Orbis Books, 2005), 29.

50   *People are increasingly on the move*: Gryboski, "Five Trends."

   People in diaspora potentially: Gryboski, "Five Trends."

51   *A church northwest of Detroit, for example*: Beth Ernest, personal correspondence with the author, August 14, 2017.

   It is often most difficult: A. Scott Moreau, Gary R. Corwin, and Gary B. McGee, *Introducing World Missions: A Biblical, Historical, and Practical Survey* (Grand Rapids: Baker Academic, 2006), 284.

52   *effectively communicate the gospel*: Bruce Riley Ashford, *Theology and Practice of Mission: God, the Church, and the Nations* (Nashville: B&H Publishing, 2011), 208.

53   *Introduction of American dress*: Christopher R. Little, "Breaking Bad Missiological Habits," in *Discovering the Mission of God: Best Missional Practices for the 21st Century,* ed. Mike Barnett and Robin Martin (Downers Grove, IL: IVP Academic, 2012), 487.

   Missionary Brett Miller described a cab ride: Brett Miller, "Do Western Missionaries Damage Culture?," *TEAM* (blog), April 15, 2014, https://team .org/blog/do-western-missionaries-damage-cultures.

54   *The task of missions may involve*: J. Rupert Morgan, "Global Trends and the North American Church in Mission: Discovering the Church's Role in the Twenty-First Century," *International Bulletin of Mission Research* 40/4 (2016): 325-38.

3 CRISIS RESPONSE AND SUSTAINABLE DEVELOPMENT

58   *Some years ago*: Portions of this story first appeared in "Should You Give Cash to a Homeless Person?," http://sharonrhoover.com/2012/12/03/how-to -care-for-the-homeless.

   Is it personal failure or a broken system: See Steve Corbett and Brian Fikkert, *When Helping Hurts: How to Alleviate Poverty Without Hurting the Poor . . . and Yourself* (Chicago: Moody Publishers, 2012), 79.

62   *SUVs have become such a problem*: Corporation of National & Community Service, *Managing Spontaneous Volunteers in Times of Disaster*, Participant

Materials: Full-Day Classroom Training, www.nationalservice.gov/sites
/default/files/resource/hon-cncs-msvtd_participant_materials.pdf.

64   *Seldom, immediate, and temporary*: Corbett and Fikkert, *When Helping
Hurts*, 104-5.

many of our well-intended efforts: Robert D. Lupton, *Toxic Charity: How
Churches and Charities Hurt Those They Help (and How to Reverse It)* (New
York: HarperCollins, 2011), 3-4.

For forty years we have been: Robert D. Lupton, *From Toxic Charity to Re-
demptive Incarnational Community* (Verge Network, 2016),
http://my.vergenetwork.org/ebook-from-toxic-charity-to-redemptive
-community-bob-lupton.

65   *Please don't build orphanages*: Founder and CEO of Every Orphan's Hope,
Gary Schneider, personal conversation with the author, August 2010.

66   *the church can be a significant partner*: Bryant L. Myers, *Walking with the
Poor: Principles and Practices of Transformational Development* (Maryknoll,
NY: Orbis Books, 2011), 317.

67   *a trusted partnership where people*: Natasha Sistrunk Robinson, *Mentor for
Life: Finding Purpose Through Intentional Discipleship* (Grand Rapids:
Zondervan, 2016), 137.

the biggest mistakes that North American churches: Corbett and Fikkert,
When Helping Hurts, 101.

68   *International Justice Mission offers a free workbook*: International Justice
Mission, *IJM Community Justice Assessment: Tool for Churches* (accessed
May 20, 2017), www.ijm.org/content/local-community-justice
-assessment-tool.

69   *sometimes we forget that even people*: Liz Sawyer, "Co-op Meets Food Desert:
Cash-Strapped Volunteers Get a Discount on Groceries," *TakePart*, October
14, 2015, www.takepart.com/article/2015/10/13/coop-meets-food-desert
-volunteers-discount-groceries.

70   *the North American need for speed*: Corbett and Fikkert, *When Helping
Hurts*, 124.

71   *We fed a thousand people today*: Corbett and Fikkert, *When Helping Hurts*,
114.

a theology of engagement in and with: James Davison Hunter, *To Change the
World* (New York: Oxford University Press, 2010), 243; see also 244-46.

72   *The best thing we can do*: David E. Fitch, *Faithful Presence: Seven Disciplines That Shape the Church for Mission* (Downers Grove, IL: InterVarsity Press, 2016), 116.

Presence precedes proclamation: Fitch, *Faithful Presence*, 107.

a call to be sure we do: Myers, *Walking with the Poor*, 310.

73   *God finds someone or a people*: Fitch, *Faithful Presence,* 204.

the goal is not to produce: Corbett and Fikkert, *When Helping Hurts*, 113.

4 TIME AND MONEY

80   *Annual self-storage revenue in the United States*: Alexander Harris, "US Self-Storage Industry Statistics," SpareFoot Storage Beat, May 23, 2017, www.sparefoot.com/self-storage/news/1432-self-storage-industry-statistics.

83   *People love to say*: Allison Kooser, "Beyond the Fishing Rod: Unlocking Innovation and Sustainable Development Goal 9," *Opportunity International* (blog), May 22, 2017, http://opportunity.org/news/blog/2017/may/beyond -the-fishing-rod-unlocking-innovation-and-sustainable-development -goal-9.

read annual financial reviews: The Christian Legal Society has an excellent guide on their website called "Evaluating a Charity's Financial Health," https://clsnet.org/page.aspx?pid=383.

84   *55 percent of millennials*: Joan Raymond, "Do You Give Time or Money? NBC Poll Finds Millennials and Boomers May Disagree," *CNBC Today*, December 1, 2015, www.cnbc.com/2015/12/01/do-you-give-time-or-money-nbc-poll -finds-millennials-and-boomers-may-disagree.html.

85   *calling members of the body of Christ 'volunteers'*: Michelle van Loon, "Church Volunteers: An Oxymoron," *CT Women*, July 2010, www .christianitytoday.com/women/2010/july/church-volunteers-oxymoron .html.

acknowledge that the Holy Spirit: Gary G. Hoag, R. Scott Rodin, and Wesley K. Willmer, *The Choice: The Christ-Centered Pursuit of Kingdom Outcomes* (Winchester, VA: ECFA Press, 2014), 86.

89   *Momma said there's only so much*: *Forrest Gump,* directed by Robert Zemeckis (Hollywood, CA: Paramount Pictures, 2001).

91   *it raised over 115 million dollars*: Katie Rogers, "The Ice Bucket Challenge Helped Scientists Discover a New Gene Tied to ALS," *New York Times*, July

27, 2016, www.nytimes.com/2016/07/28/health/the-ice-bucket-challenge
-helped-scientists-discover-a-new-gene-tied-to-als.html.

91   *willingness to contribute to a charitable*: Christopher Y. Olivola and Eldar
      Shafir, "The Martyrdom Effect: When Pain and Effort Increase Prosocial
      Contributions," *Journal of Behavioral Decision Making* 26/1 (January 2013),
      http://onlinelibrary.wiley.com/doi/10.1002/bdm.767/full.

92   *Imagine how stunning it would be*: Richard Stearns, *The Hole in Our Gospel:
      What Does God Expect of Us? The Answer That Changed My Life and Might
      Just Change the World* (Nashville: Thomas Nelson, 2009), 219.

5 BENEFITS AND DRAWBACKS
OF SHORT-TERM TEAMS

100   *The twenty-first-century North American church*: J. Rupert Morgan, "Global
      Trends and the North American Church in Mission: Discovering the Church's
      Role in the Twenty-First Century," *International Bulletin of Mission Research*
      40/4 (2016): 325-38.

101   *can enhance our ability to interact*: David A. Livermore, *Serving with Eyes
      Wide Open: Doing Short-Term Missions with Cultural Intelligence* (Grand
      Rapids: Baker Books, 2013), 111.

      The guilt-innocence culture of my Western: An excellent resource to explore
      worldviews and the gospel is Jayson Georges, *The 3D Gospel: Ministry in
      Guilt, Shame, and Fear Cultures* (Time Press, 2014).

102   *Many people said it was one*: Jenny Gordon, correspondence with the author,
      September 1, 2017.

106   *A highly respected organization equips*: Steve Corbett and Brian Fikkert,
      When Helping Hurts (Chicago: Moody Publishers, 2012), 161.

      churches include STMs in their annual: Morgan, "Global Trends," 325-38.

      In the current climate of decreasing: See the recent Barna report published in
      partnership with Thrivent Financial, *The Generosity Gap* (Ventura, CA:
      Barna Group, 2017), 8.

      Throughout the decade of the 1970s: Brian M. Howell, *Short-Term Mission:
      An Ethnography of Christian Travel Narrative and Experience* (Downers
      Grove, IL: IVP Academic, 2012), 100.

107   *In doing so, however, they harm*: Corbett and Fikkert, *When Helping Hurts*,
      64.

110   *our guiding narrative should be*: Howell, *Short-Term Mission*, 214.

110   *On the basis of relationship*: Howell, *Short-Term Mission*, 214.

113   *while it is true that short-term mission*: Howell, *Short-Term Mission*, 201.

6 SERVING THE UNDISCIPLED AND DISCIPLING THE SERVANT

121   *of all the classical Spiritual Disciplines*: Richard J. Foster, *Celebration of Discipline: The Path to Spiritual Growth* (New York: HarperCollins, 1988), 126, 130.

124   *80 percent of those who attend church*: Joe Carter, "Study: Most Churchgoers Never Share the Gospel," The Gospel Coalition, August 30, 2012, www .thegospelcoalition.org/article/study-most-churchgoers-never-share-the -gospel.

7 MINIMIZING AND EMBRACING RISK

135   *Are you caught in the enchantment*: John Piper, *Risk Is Right: Better to Lose Your Life Than to Waste It* (Wheaton, IL: Crossway, 2013), 38.

136   *not heroism, or the lust for adventure*: Piper, *Risk Is Right,* 39.

139   *When called by God to unsafe places*: Anna E. Hampton, *Facing Danger: A Guide Through Risk* (New Prague, MN: Zendagi Press, 2016), 127.

141   *The Holy Spirit's leading is the one*: Hampton, *Facing Danger*, 68.

       Instead, our primary focus here: Hampton, *Facing Danger*, 68.

142   *one well-known risk assessment model*: Hampton, *Facing Danger*, 122.

143   *Wherever people love each other*: Frederick Buechner, "Wherever People Love Each Other," May 17, 2016, www.frederickbuechner.com/blog/2016/5/17 /wherever-people-love-each-other.

       There are noticeably fewer travelers: Margot Starbuck, *Small Things with Great Love* (Downers Grove, IL: InterVarsity Press, 2011), 87.

CONCLUSION: MOBILIZING OUR CONGREGATIONS

149   *Many resources are available to help*: Missions coaching organizations, such as Sixteen:Fifteen Coaching and The Outreach Foundation, come alongside churches to guide them toward a focused, Spirit-led strategy. Aubrey Malphurs, *Advanced Strategic Planning: A 21st Century Model for Church and Mission Leaders,* 3rd edition (Grand Rapids: Baker Books, 2013), offers a well-researched model to guide a church through a nine-step development and implementation process. Gary C. Hoag, R. Scott Rodin, and Wesley K.

Wilmer, *The Choice: The Christ-Centered Pursuit of Kingdom Outcomes* (ECFA Press, 2014) helps articulate end goals for ministry outcomes. John Mark Terry and J. D. Payne, *Developing a Strategy for Missions: A Biblical, Historical, and Cultural Introduction* (Grand Rapids: Baker Academic, 2013) provides valuable historical context along with cultural assessments to establish a biblically based missions strategy. Questionnaires, worksheets, and checklists offer valuable insights for the process.

150 *When studying, ask many questions*: For more on conducting cultural research, see Terry and Payne, *Developing a Strategy for Missions*. See also Jayson Georges, *The 3D Gospel: Ministry in Guilt, Shame, and Fear Cultures* (Time Press, 2014), which clarifies the roles of guilt, shame, and honor worldviews on the presentation and understanding of the gospel message.

While the goal of educating: Gary Haugen and Victor Boutros, *The Locust Effect: Why the End of Poverty Requires the End of Violence* (New York: Oxford University Press, 2015).

151 *There are numerous tools available*: SurveyMonkey (surveymonkey.com) is an easy-to-use website with free templates, including well-written gifts and talents surveys.

152 *raise their members' awareness*: Robert D. Lupton, *Toxic Charity: How Churches and Charities Hurt Those They Help (and How to Reverse It)* (New York: HarperCollins, 2011), 74.

When planning one route: These ideas first appeared in *The State of Pastors: How Today's Faith Leaders Are Navigating Life and Leadership in an Age of Complexity* (Ventura, CA: Barna Group, 2017), 112-13. Used by permission.

154 *Tom Sine writes about the ways God*: Tom Sine, *The New Conspirators: Creating the Future One Mustard Seed at a Time* (Downers Grove, IL: InterVarsity Press, 2008).

155 *There needs to be a radical*: Phill Butler, "Is Our Collaboration for the Kingdom Effective?," *Lausanne Global Analysis* 6/1 (January 2017), www.lausanne.org/content/lga/2017-01/is-our-collaboration-for-the-kingdom-effective.

The 21st century has witnessed: Center for the Study of Global Christianity, *Christianity in Its Global Context, 1970-2020: Society, Religion, and Mission* (South Hamilton, MA: Gordon-Conwell Theological Seminary, 2013), 76, www.gordonconwell.edu/ockenga/research/documents/christianityinitsglobalcontext.pdf.

155   *Globalization is allowing the proliferation*: Stan Guthrie, "Global Report: Past Midnight," *Evangelical Missions Quarterly* 36/1 (2000): 98-104.

160   *The great thing is to prevent*: C. S. Lewis, *The Screwtape Letters* (New York: Touchstone, 1996), 57.

APPENDIX 1

167   The ideas presented in this appendix first appeared in *The State of Pastors: How Today's Faith Leaders Are Navigating Life and Leadership in an Age of Complexity* (Ventura, CA: Barna Group, 2017), 112-13. Used by permission.

God has called us to ministry. But it's not enough to have a vision for ministry if you don't have the practical skills for it. Nor is it enough to do the work of ministry if what you do is headed in the wrong direction. We need both vision *and* expertise for effective ministry. We need *praxis*.

Praxis puts theory into practice. It brings cutting-edge ministry expertise from visionary practitioners. You'll find sound biblical and theological foundations for ministry in the real world, with concrete examples for effective action and pastoral ministry. Praxis books are more than the "how to" – they're also the "why to." And because *being* is every bit as important as *doing*, Praxis attends to the inner life of the leader as well as the outer work of ministry. Feed your soul, and feed your ministry.

If you are called to ministry, you know you can't do it on your own. Let Praxis provide the companions you need to equip God's people for life in the kingdom.

www.ivpress.com/praxis

flooding back. He hadn't felt this way since he'd been with Ellie. He decided that it was time for them to fly back to the cliff and spend some time together.

"Come on," he said to Becky. "Let's go and find somewhere quiet."

Holly, Ricky and all Becky's friends could see that Peter and Becky were going to be very happy together.

When Becky and Peter landed on the clifftop, they just stared at each other. Peter thought about Grandad's last words after the tragic loss of Ellie. He'd been certain that one day Peter would be happy again and of course Grandad had been absolutely right. It was just so sad that he wasn't here to see it for himself.

The two puffins spent the rest of the day together wandering along the clifftop, chatting to each other. At the end of the day before flying out to spend their first night together on the water, they made a promise to each other.

"Becky," Peter said. "I want you to be my special puffin and I'll do all that I can to protect you for the rest of my life."

"Thank you, Peter," Becky replied. "I can think of nothing better than spending the rest of my life with you."

The two puffins spent the rest of the day together wandering along the cliff-top, chatting to each other.

They did some bill tapping and then flew out to sea. The next morning they returned to the cliff top. They found Holly and Ricky.

"Becky and I have got something to tell you," Peter started to explain.

"You don't need to say anything," Holly interrupted. "We can see that you two are going to be as happy together as Ricky and I."

Becky and Peter looked at each other and smiled.

"Congratulations! Peter, it really is great to see that things have worked out at last," Holly replied. "I just knew that you would eventually find happiness."

The four of them did some bill tapping.

Peter thought again about Grandad. What a wise old puffin! He was never wrong!

Chapter Seven: A New Challenge

Peter decided there was no time to be lost in preparing for pufflings now that he'd found his special female puffin. He explained to Becky about Grandad's wish that they use his old burrow.

"Grandad was a very wise puffin," Peter said. "He used to talk about all sorts of things and seemed to know a lot. Sadly, he decided that last year would be his last here on the clifftop. He gave me his old burrow. Finding new sites for burrows isn't easy, so I'm really glad he did."

"He must've been a very special puffin," Becky added.

They waddled along the clifftop together looking for the burrow. Peter was a little worried in case someone else had decided to move in already. As it happened he needn't have worried because the burrow looked most uninviting. The roof at the entrance had collapsed completely.

"Oh!" Peter said as he looked at the burrow, "Grandad did warn me that repairs might be needed, but this looks quite serious. I didn't think that we'd have to rebuild it."

"Never mind," Becky said. "If we take it in turns I'm sure we'll have the repairs completed in no time."

Peter decided that he should start. He wanted to show Becky that he could do the repairs without her help. He attacked the pile of earth very enthusiastically, doing whatever he could to shovel the earth out of the way. Becky had to retreat to a safe distance to watch his efforts because she was being showered with all sorts of bits and pieces.

When Peter stopped for a rest, his appearance had changed dramatically. His colourful beak and beautiful white front were now completely brown. He coughed and spluttered as he tried to get the dirt out of his mouth and his eyes.

"You do look funny," Becky couldn't help giggling. She certainly looked very cute when she giggled.

Peter didn't think it was that funny! After all he'd been working very hard.

When he could see again, he was pleased to notice that he'd made some progress. He could actually see into the burrow. The collapse at the entrance had looked more serious than it really was. He was about to continue digging when he was interrupted by Becky.

"My turn!" she announced.

Peter hadn't expected her to volunteer quite so quickly but he wanted to clean himself and so he decided to let her have a go.

"OK," he replied.

Becky wasn't quite as energetic as Peter and progress was a lot slower. It didn't take Peter long to become impatient. He wandered up behind her and opened his mouth to say something but never started the sentence.

At that moment Becky managed to heave a particularly large clod of earth in Peter's direction. It wedged itself firmly in his mouth. Having recovered from the shock and removed the piece of earth from his mouth, Peter decided to keep out of the way and say nothing.

Becky may not have worked as quickly as Peter but she was very thorough and the blockage was soon cleared.

"I think we can go in now," she remarked.

Peter peered into the burrow. He seemed satisfied that it was safe to go inside.

"All right," he said. "Follow me!"

He waddled into the burrow fairly cautiously, as he wasn't sure what he might find. Becky followed him. They continued along the tunnel until they reached the nesting chamber. Peter thought it looked fine, but Becky seemed to be rather particular about cleanliness.

"I can see that some tidying up is needed," she said looking round the chamber. "We'll have to give it a good clean."

Peter was going to make a remark about her being very fussy, but decided not to. They turned round and left the burrow.

"I'll start doing some clearing out then," Peter volunteered.

"Fine!" Becky replied. "I'll wait out here."

As he was waddling along the tunnel towards the nesting chamber, something caught Peter's attention. There seemed to have been some repairs to part of the wall. It looked to him as if someone had blocked up what could have been another tunnel.

"Time to investigate!" Peter thought.

As it turned out, this was not a good idea. As with most of Peter's thinking, he really didn't think carefully enough!

Peter decided that investigating a second tunnel was much more exciting than cleaning a nesting chamber!

He carefully scraped away the earth. Sure enough there was a passage going sideways. It was quite narrow.

"This could be very interesting," Peter thought.

It never occurred to him that Grandad may have blocked this passage off for a special reason. Peter waddled along the side tunnel and came to a junction with a much wider tunnel where he could turn either left or right.

He turned right and soon found himself face to face with a very angry puffin who was obviously the owner of the burrow that Peter had entered. Peter just managed to turn round before being chased out of the tunnel by the puffin who didn't like uninvited visitors.

Becky couldn't understand what had happened. Peter had gone into one burrow and was now being chased out of another one!

"Peter!" she said when the angry puffin had returned to its burrow. "What's going on?"

Peter had a rather sore bottom where he had been pecked several times by the angry puffin. He then had to explain to Becky how he'd decided to do some exploring instead of cleaning the nesting chamber.

"I don't know why there's a tunnel connecting the two burrows," he said, "but I think Grandad must've blocked it off to stop his pufflings wandering into trouble,"

"It didn't stop you wandering into trouble, did it?" Becky replied.

"No!" Peter responded rather sheepishly, realising how silly he'd been.

"Perhaps it might be an idea if you blocked it up again," Becky suggested.

Peter agreed. Things were not going according to plan. He went back into the tunnel and blocked up the tunnel to the neighbouring burrow. Once this had been done, he came out of the burrow. He'd had enough for the moment. Luckily Becky was quite happy to take over for the time being.

She went into the nesting chamber where she gathered up all sorts of bits and pieces. These she then brought out of the burrow. Peter was quite happy to watch, as Becky seemed very content with what she was doing. Eventually she thought the nesting chamber was tidy enough.

"Come and see!" she said to Peter. "I think you'll notice a difference."

Peter followed her into the burrow. The nesting chamber did look very clean. Peter was very impressed.

"Well done," he said. "It looks very nice. I think we need to get some fresh bits and pieces so that the nest will be more comfortable for sitting on."

"Let's go and see what we can find then," Becky suggested.

Once outside, they went their separate ways looking for suitable items. Peter found another magnificent large feather very like the one he'd tried to give to Sally. He was sure that this would be ideal for the nesting chamber. He carried it back to the burrow, but then found he had a problem.

When he tried to carry it into the tunnel, the feather refused to go because it seemed to be too wide. No matter how he tried it simply would not go through the entrance. Meanwhile Becky had returned and could see that Peter was having a problem.

When he tried to carry it into the tunnel, the feather refused to go because it seemed to be too wide.

"What a lovely feather!" was her first remark.

Peter put the feather on the ground.

"For some reason," he said, "it won't go into the tunnel."

This puzzled Becky as well. When Peter had put the feather on the ground, he'd placed it pointing in the direction of the tunnel. Looking at it in that position, it seemed that it would fit quite easily. When Becky picked up the feather and waddled towards the entrance, the feather had turned round and like Peter there was no way she could make it fit through the entrance.

Becky then put it down again in the same way that Peter had done. Both puffins looked at the feather and looked at the entrance. They felt certain that it should go in. Peter picked up the feather and tried again. When he reached the entrance to the burrow, the feather seemed to have turned itself round again and refused to go into the tunnel.

"I just don't understand," Peter said when he'd put the feather down again.

"Nor do I!" Becky added. "It's a pity because it's a lovely feather."

The feather had defeated them, so Peter carefully removed it from the entrance to the burrow and gave up any idea of taking it into the nesting chamber. They did find other smaller bits and pieces. Eventually both puffins were happy with the work they'd done.

"I think Grandad's burrow looks great," Peter commented.

"So do I!" Becky replied.

Peter looked at Becky and smiled. She was very beautiful. She didn't seem to mind that he'd made a fool of himself earlier. He was also quite sure she would make a wonderful mother for their pufflings.

"Come on, let's go and find some food," he said as they tapped bills.

Over the next few days the two puffins took time to enjoy each other's company. Becky continued to make small alterations inside the burrow. Peter smiled at this. He couldn't understand why she needed everything to be quite so perfect.

As the days passed he noticed that Becky appeared to be putting on weight. It didn't worry him, but he couldn't understand why. It wasn't long before he discovered the reason. He'd returned from one of his fishing trips. Becky, instead of coming to greet him, called to him from inside the burrow.

"Peter!" she cried out excitedly, "Come and see what's happened."

Peter waddled along the tunnel and into the nesting chamber. Becky got up from where she was sitting. What was there? An egg!

"Oh Becky!" Peter exclaimed. "What a surprise! You're brilliant!"

"I'm so excited!" she replied with a lovely smile.

Peter was very proud of Becky. He had no idea why Becky had suddenly decided to lay an egg, but he knew that pufflings came from eggs. This was what had made him so excited. Their first puffling would soon arrive!

He realised that fishing and egg sitting duties would have to be shared with Becky from now on. He waddled back out into the sunshine and took a moment to think about what had happened. There'd been lots of ups and downs in his short life, but he was very happy. He now had to show Becky that he could be a responsible parent.

Over the next few days Becky spent most of her time sitting on the egg but Peter was very happy to take over so that she could have a break and do some fishing. At night Becky stayed in the burrow while Peter joined his friends out at sea.

It was a busy time for the male puffins in the colony because most of the females had laid eggs that needed looking after. In fact, Peter and Becky had been one of the last pairs of puffins to produce an egg. Holly had laid an egg quite a few days before Becky.

Gradually news that eggs were hatching and pufflings were arriving began to circulate among Peter's group of friends. Even Ricky managed to look excited when Holly's egg hatched.

"Please tell Holly that I'm really happy for her," Peter said when Ricky told him the news.

"I will," Ricky replied.

Soon after this Peter began to worry. He realised that Becky's egg was just about the only egg that hadn't hatched. He decided to ask her about it.

"Becky," he said when he next returned to the burrow, "are you at all worried about the egg?"

"No!" She replied slightly alarmed. "Why should I be worried?"

"It seems that everybody else's egg has hatched," Peter explained, "but yours hasn't."

"Oh!" She said looking at the egg.

"Is there something we ought to do?" Peter asked.

"I don't think so," Becky replied. "I'm keeping the egg warm. I'm sure there's nothing else we can do."

Over the next few days Peter's worries increased. There was still no sign of the egg hatching. He didn't want to worry Becky again, but he'd heard about eggs that hadn't hatched. The puffins had been forced to roll these eggs out of their burrows and over the edge of the cliff.

He thought he should ask Ricky for Holly's advice, as she always seemed to know what was best.

When Peter next saw Ricky, he told him that he was worried about the egg.

"Ricky, can you please ask Holly what I should do?" Peter said. "I'm very worried."

Ricky came back later that day with a message from Holly.

"Holly says that you should wait two more days," Ricky explained. "Your egg was one of the last to appear. She says that if it hasn't hatched by then, there is something wrong."

Another day passed. When Peter returned to the burrow, still nothing had happened.

Peter stayed at sea fishing for the whole of the next day. He realised that the time had come to tell Becky that there was something wrong with the egg and they would have to get rid of it. He was very upset because he was so looking forward to their first puffling.

He landed outside the burrow and waddled down the tunnel. When he arrived in the nesting chamber, Becky was fast asleep sitting on the egg. She looked so lovely and Peter didn't know how to tell her what they were going to have to do.

She woke up with a start and it wasn't because Peter had appeared! Something was happening underneath her!

"Look, Peter!" she said as she moved off the egg.

Peter had a look and noticed that at last a small hole had appeared in the egg. Together they stared at the egg.

This puffling was about to make up for lost time!

Cr … rack!

The egg suddenly broke in two to reveal a beautiful fluffy puffling.

At last Becky and Peter had become Mother Puffin and Father Puffin!

The egg suddenly broke in two to reveal a beautiful fluffy puffling.